JUST GO SELL!

A PRACTICAL GUIDE TO SUCCESSFUL SELLING

COLIN KNOWLES

I'd just like to thank the continued support from my wife Jennifer who's encouragement inspired me to start, process and finish this book.

CONTENTS

INTRODUCTION   VII

THE MODERN PROSPECT.
"JUST LOOKING, THANKS!"   1

ATTITUDE   10

PROFESSIONALISM   21

MAKE A FRIEND, LEARN THE
LINGO, MAKE THE SALE!   33

SMART SELLING   40

GREAT QUESTIONING   47

RELATIONSHIP STRENGTHENING   57

HANDLING OBJECTIONS   60

WHY BUY THIS?   67

BASIC SALES SKILLS AND CLOSING TECHNIQUES   76

BODY LANGUAGE   94

THE OVERVIEW   101

VALUE, EXCITEMENT, AND URGENCY   105

ASKING FOR THE BUSINESS   115

THE FOUR PILLARS OF SELLING   120

PUTTING IT ALL TOGETHER   127

A FEW FINAL THOUGHTS   141

ABOUT THE AUTHOR   147

INTRODUCTION

Why read this book?

Maybe you're a seasoned sales executive or perhaps new to the industry. Maybe you're considering a move into sales or starting a home business that's sales dependent. Possibly you're a company owner or a sales manager accountable for a team.

Whatever your position in sales, there is one thing we all should have in common—the desire to improve. The reason you're reading this book is your awareness that there's room for progression and growth in your sales performance.

Congratulations, you've realized no one is going to wave a magic wand and, *hey presto,* you're a dynamic selling machine. The very fact that you're reading this book deserves recognition because you're doing something to help you achieve your sales goals. There is no graduation in sales, and there's never a level that can be achieved that means you've gone as far as you can go.

Success in sales is about continuous performance improvement through self-development and attitude. In short, you have to want to achieve and win to be successful in sales. You've taken the first step in attaining this through your self-motivation in reading this book.

In this book, you'll not find complex neurological sales theories or scientific equations as to why people buy. There are no in-depth confusing psychological formulas that try to reinvent the sales process. Oh, and no hypnotizing either.

What you will find are solid, practical, and dynamic approaches to the sales process that are simple to understand and digest. You'll gain confidence, credibility, and a fresh approach to sales aimed at successfully closing today's modern prospect.

Whether you sell door to door, lead source, telesales, royalty selling, network marketing, podium selling, or any other form of sales, welcome!

You've read this far, so stay motivated and keep going. Launch your sales potential, and increase your closing percentage and income.

MAYBE TOMORROW? BETTER TODAY!

THE MODERN PROSPECT. "JUST LOOKING, THANKS!"

How do you feel when you go into a shop and the sales assistant approaches and asks, "Can I help you?" Most of us usually reply, "No, I'm just looking, thanks," then hope he or she goes away, even if we really do need help or are interested in buying something.

How about when the phone call you've just picked up is a telesales pitch? Does "Now's not a good time" come to mind?

Maybe one of your friends has just started a new home business selling nutritional products and is so excited to tell you all about it, especially how much it costs and how great it would be if you joined, too. How irritating is that?

I was on a beach in Spain, and the temperature was soaring hot. There wasn't a bar, restaurant, or water facility for refreshment nearby. A man walked along the beach carrying an ice bucket full of cool, refreshing drinks, offering them for sale. He went from person to person and hardly sold a drink. Most people rudely waved a hand as to shoo him away like an irritating fly. The cliché "Couldn't sell water to a thirsty man" sprang to mind.

Why is this? Why do we make ourselves so close minded that we never give ourselves a chance to be open to suggestion that the product or service being offered might just benefit us?

The fact is that none of us like to be sold. The idea that someone can invade our space and leave us with something we don't really need does not go down well. So much so that we deliberately make up excuses to make them go away. As consumers, we like to feel as though *we* make the choice to buy. It was our decision on the color, size, style, or service.

"If the salesperson at that other place hadn't been so pushy, we'd have bought there. Instead, we bought the same thing right here. The reason is simply that the person we bought from was really friendly and helpful." We've all heard that one before, maybe even done it before, but why? Exactly the same product, probably even the same price, yet something has influenced us to buy somewhere else from someone else.

This consumer mentality has been around for years. One of the greatest joys of buying a product should be the actual sales process. You can take this one stage further and add that the pre-purchase experience is the deciding factor of whether we buy it or not. The relationship with the salesperson and the manner of how he or she responds or interacts with us can be a deciding factor whether we buy or not.

TODAY'S MODERN PROSPECT

Today's prospect certainly has changed. Never before has so much information been readily available at the flick of a page or click of a button. Opinions, forums, in-depth insights, reviews, and existing consumer opinions are there for all to see in a second.

Smartphones, laptops, and tablets all with instant access to dozens of Internet search engines make research on a product simply a finger swipe away.

From a salesperson's point of view, is this a good thing? Some may argue that the prospect already knows what he or she wants and that sales skills could become a thing of the past. The case could be made that we are heading toward a vending machine society with an "insert credit card here" attitude, where personal contact from a representative is no longer necessary.

If this were the case, why does industry still invest so much money into customer care and sales training? Why do many of the listed Fortune 500 companies still insist that interactive relationships create sales opportunities?

Online companies invest millions on how their website visually appears and appeals. Their wording is very carefully chosen and the "Contact Us" tab is clearly indicated to ensure the visitor has an option to interact with a representative. Many online businesses don't wait for the visitor to click the "Contact Us" tab, and instead they have an automatic pop-up window promoting an instant, real-time, live interaction with a representative. Why bother if we are truly in a vending machine society?

Telephone-automated directing programs prompting the caller to "Press one" for this and "Press two" for that can be very annoying, impersonal, and incredibly frustrating. When a human voice eventually picks up the telephone (following what appeared to be an eternity of pressing the numeric pad on the telephone and being redirected to several wrong submenus) finally gives a great sense of relief.

Not everyone likes to buy online. Some prefer to take their purchase with them once they have parted with their hard-earned cash. They prefer not to track their goods over the coming days and hope the neighbor is available to sign for it (as they will not be at home) when the parcel is delivered.

Some purchasers think it's good to physically see and touch the product before buying. This is especially the case if the goods are clothing, shoes, or something that is personal to size or taste. It is much easier to swap while you are physically at the location instead of the headache of mailing it back and receiving a replacement a few days later, only to be disappointed again.

In these times of credit card and ID fraud, there are still many reluctant to part with sensitive information or card details online. They prefer to be present at the point of sale, tap their PIN number in the machine secretly, then safely replace their card where it came from.

Finally, for some, good old face-to-face interaction is much more comfortable. There are many reasons consumers still buy offline and will continue to do so. Millions of dollars are still spent building shopping malls, outlets, and department stores and even more is spent when the doors finally open.

TOO MUCH INFORMATION?

As a consumer, if you browse independent Internet forums relating to a particular product you're interested in, the majority of the posts you find can be quite negative. They tend to take a more critical approach to what the product doesn't do.

For example, if you've just bought a car, and it totally satisfied your expectations, would you be bothered to go online and search for a relevant forum and tell everyone just how good it is? Probably not because you couldn't be bothered—it works, it's great, and you got what you paid for.

However, if you just bought the car, and it was nothing but trouble, and the backup service provided was as poor as the cars performance, would you then go online and search for a forum and have your say? Probably, as you're disgruntled and now have the motivation to do so.

There are literally thousands of Internet consumer sites that provide reviews and personal opinions of virtually every product or service available. If you type a product into an Internet search engine, pages of links appear and are accessible with the swipe of a finger.

With so much instant information available to us, are we in a world of informed consumers, or is there simply too much information?

Too much information can lead to confusion. With hundreds of Internet "advisor" sites riddled with conflicting opinions, can we really make an informed decision on which product is the right one for us?

Today, are we in a world of well-informed or well-confused consumers? There is a saying that a person with one watch knows the exact time, a person with two isn't quite sure.

Most consumers do some Internet research on products before buying. This does not mean they are ready to buy, as they have all the facts and no further questions need answering. It simply means they have explored some of the pros and cons of the product and have some knowledge they might not have had access to several years ago.

With this new information, the modern prospect may have a *better idea* of the product they require. This will enable them to converse more effectively with the sales representative regarding its usage and limitations against that of a competitor.

The purchase decision can be hugely influenced by a professional sales consultant who can transparently guide the prospect with confidence through the maze created by conflicting and confusing reports on Internet forums and other readily available sources.

SALES EXECUTIVE OR PROFESSIONAL CONSULTANT?

The modern prospect certainly needs a new approach when it comes to selling. He or she has had a bad sales experience or two, perhaps feeling really pressured into buying something and had the cold shoulder from the salesperson when he or she declined the offer.

The prospect has had the insistent telesales call, where it's now or never, then been inconveniently recalled with a better offer from the one he or she previously declined.

These examples have contributed to the image and perception that some people hold toward the sales profession. We (salespeople) have been regarded as untrustworthy, dishonest, and it's all about the commission and what's in it for us.

It is our responsibility to adapt and rebrand our image from being a "pushy salesperson" to that of a professional consultant. "What's in it for us?" will no longer happen until "What's in it for them?" becomes the first and most important priority.

TRUST AND CONFIDENCE

The modern prospect needs to feel trust and have confidence in you as a person and believe in your abilities.

Let's take an example of this. A consultant surgeon needs to gain the confidence and trust of his or her patient way before treatment starts. They will meet by appointment, and it's safe to say the patient is nervous and probably confused. The credentials of the surgeon will be discussed to demonstrate that the patient is in the safest possible hands. This is the first step toward gaining the patient's confidence.

The consultant needs to be 100 percent confident he or she fully understands the patient's symptoms to enable a correct diagnosis and treatment required. The surgeon explains to the patient that it's necessary to ask several questions as to his or her suffering— where it is, type of pain, frequency of the pain, how long he or she has been feeling this way, and a multitude of relative questions. The patient will gladly answer these questions and is probably thankful to be with someone who appears to care and wishes to appreciate his or her condition.

Talking the patient through the diagnosis questioning stage is a big part of the consultant's job, as it demonstrates his or her ability to listen and understand. This, in turn, gives more confidence and reassurance to the patient.

The newly gained confidence is taken one stage further as treatment is explained thoroughly with the patient. The consultant ensures the patient completely understands exactly what will happen, why it needs to happen, the risks, the recovery period, and any other treatment that may follow.

Confidence, trust, and belief in the surgeon's ability is of paramount importance to the patient, as a very delicate decision must be made whether to continue with the recommended procedure.

Surgeons and other such professional consultants are regarded and respected very highly, and their suggestions for solutions are usually followed.

In these days of private medicine, isn't it fair to say that a consultant surgeon is in the sales industry, selling services to the patient? After all, the patient does have a choice of who to use for treatment. The surgeon does earn a fee for consultancy and surgery performed, and isn't this the same as a sales commission?

He or she is not deemed as money-grabbing, what's in it for me, cheap-shot salespeople we would normally avoid, but why not?

Confidence, trust, belief, and transparency are the difference. The patient felt the surgeon understood him or her completely. The surgeon's recommendations made sense, and his or her specialist knowledge added credibility.

In the sales industry, we need to have the same effect with our prospects as the consultant surgeon achieves with patients. We must replace the prospect's current expectation of having to endure a high-pressured sales environment with a now or never pitch.

Sure, we want to make the sale today, and the title of this book reflects that. As you read, be open to making some simple changes.

Consider new ideas on sales techniques and how you can more effectively approach the point of sale.

In sales, just like the surgeon, we need to become recognized as professional consultants. This is much more than just changing your title on the business card; *it is earned.*

This book's observations and suggestions can assist your efforts in becoming a more credible and respected professional consultant. Your sales figures should increase and generate sales with less effort and desperate convincing.

You should feel confident and in control during sales presentations and quickly gain trust from your prospects. To gain the most from this book, do not glance over or skim any part of it.

Get comfortable being out of your comfort zone. Try different ideas and practice them, so you gain confidence in your delivery.

Feel proud of your profession; sales is a rewarding and enjoyable career. The better you get, the more enjoyable it becomes.

ATTITUDE

There are many components and building blocks essential to becoming a professional consultant. Some components require preparation, some can be added when required, and others are essential in every presentation. These components fall under two main channels: self-development and skills development.

Self-development is all about you as a person. The first impression the prospect has is the first time he or she either meets you or talks with you over the phone. The effect that has on the prospect is virtually irreversible; you never get a second chance to make a first impression.

Skills development is bringing up to speed dated sales skills and implementing new ones acceptable by the modern prospect. It focuses on verbal and nonverbal communication and how to effectively project them to have maximum benefit.

First, we are going to look at a personal development aspect: attitude.

You may have read, listened to, or seen lifestyle gurus insisting you must always have a great attitude. You may disagree and think attitude is a waste of time and has no effect, so why bother?

One of the consequences of being human is that we have emotions. It is natural that on occasion we get out of bed on the wrong side and can be rather grumpy. Some days are better than others; however, it is up to us to control our attitude as it certainly affects and influences others around us.

I certainly don't promote flinging yourself out of bed every morning, throwing your arms in the air, and screaming, "Today will be fantastic but not as good as tomorrow," but hey, if it works for you, go for it. The one thing I will insist on is your A1 attitude during challenging times and most importantly in the sales arena.

The fact is, attitude is the one thing you can never escape. Every action you make projects an attitude—how you comb your hair, how you close the car door, how you walk, how you talk, how you eat, and so on. People make character judgments by the way you project your attitude. As you may never hide your attitude, it is vital you learn how to control it. Used the correct way, attitude is a tremendous asset that will change even the coldest of prospective clients. It will transform your outlook, your motivation, your enthusiasm, your confidence, and increase your chance of making the sale.

It will ensure your personality radiates and has a positive effect on everyone you meet. A great attitude carries a very persuasive and influencing energy. A positive attitude is very contagious. Once you project consistently a positive attitude, others around you will warm to it. Remember, your attitude is constantly being perceived and received by others. Never forget, repetition results in habit. Get in the habit of having a great attitude, and it will reward you tenfold.

Never allow yourself to be influenced by negative people or situations. So, as far as sales are concerned, negativity is a direct route to career meltdown. The single and most dangerous enemy to any professional consultant is negativity. It eliminates any foundation or building blocks to successful selling.

Do not allow yourself to be drawn into negative thinking or negative conversation, as it leads to a negative attitude. Negativity is dangerously contagious. If you start to think negative, you will dwell on it. Blame will start to emerge instead of opportunity. It will become normal to search for a reason to give up on the prospect instead of having the desire in finding a solution and a sale opening.

Perhaps the reason people run over hot coals and perform strange morning rituals is because they do want a positive attitude but don't know how to achieve it and how to maintain it.

So, we are going to cover attitude and what it takes to make a great attitude. We are going to look at how to create it, how to command it at will, and how to make it work for you in your professional and everyday life.

There are three different attributes that create a great attitude.

MIND-SET

The first of these steps is your mind-set. A positive mind-set is the starting point of gaining a great attitude. It is the spark that starts the engine, the match that starts the fire. Without it, there is no platform to build a great attitude.

A poor mind-set will not allow the development of a great attitude. A poor mind-set is only created and prolonged by the individual. It is negative and easy to harvest. Maybe you had an argument with a loved one the night before, or the car wouldn't start this morning, or the alarm didn't go off, or maybe the kids are acting up. There are many excuses we can use to justify a poor and negative mind-set. A poor mind-set will result in a lack of motivation, interest, enthusiasm, affect your listening skills, produce a lack of confidence, and lead to a lack of productivity and laziness.

Repetition forms habit. If you continue a poor mind-set, it will become second nature to have one. A poor mind-set will never change a situation. A poor mind-set has never created a winner. A poor mind-set has never created a sale. A poor mind-set will never positively influence your closing percentage and increase your earnings; it will make it worse.

Have you ever heard of a winner with a poor mind-set? Do the athletes who line up for 100-meter sprint at the Olympic Games have a poor mind-set when they hear "On your marks?" Do you think they have mentally trained and focused to accept silver? One of the reasons they are in the final is due to their positive mind-set.

Ability is what you are capable of doing. Motivation determines if you do it. Attitude determines how well you do it.

How do we create a positive mind-set, and how do we keep it? What I am about to share with you needs practice. It will become easier as you practice because it will eventually become habit. This is a great exercise you can do, and if you work at it, a healthy, positive mind-set can be called at an instant.

The first time you try this, go somewhere quiet where you cannot be disturbed. Relax, take deep breaths. It is nearly impossible to clear your mind of any thoughts, so the easiest way is to focus on positive thoughts and imagery.

Start thinking about a time in your life when you felt elated. Maybe it was your wedding day or when you saw your bride walk down the aisle or maybe when you saw your first-born child or when you passed your driving test.

Start thinking about a time when you were a winner, maybe when you sank that thirty-foot putt to win the game or maybe when you passed that exam. Maybe it was clinching that last sale and the sensation you experienced when the prospect agreed. Think of a time when you attained something like a trophy. Focus on that elation, relive the moment. Remember the sensation, and feel it again. Think about the environment on that day, visualize the sights.

We're going to introduce a technique known as a "trigger." A trigger is something you physically do that will train your mind to allow you feel that elated emotion instantly at any time (with practice).

Try this—once you have that elation in your mind, press your thumb and forefinger together on your left hand. Press them together firmly, and concentrate on that elated sensation. Feel the emotion and joy of that moment. Practice this many times, pinching your thumb and forefinger together firmly. Eventually, your mind relates to the pinching of the thumb and forefinger together as a trigger for you to feel the elation instantly. This needs constant practice, so do not give up.

Just before you meet a prospect, you have the ability to instantly attain the perfect mind-set. Simply pinch your thumb and forefinger together to trigger that emotion.

The mind-set is achieving a positive state of mind to begin with. It is displacing your mind of all negativity and achieving a positive readiness zone. Having a great mind-set is the first step to having a great positive mental attitude.

POSITIVE THINKING

Having a fantastic mind-set is one thing, prolonging it is another. A drop of fuel in an engine will start it, but it will soon stall once the fuel is used up. The next step is to ensure a steady supply of positive fuel to maintain your mind-set.

Commit to positive thinking. Make it a daily routine, stay positive, and surround yourself with positive people and positive activities. Browse Internet search engines daily for motivational quotes. Be inspired, and you will inspire.

Positive thinking will fuel your great mind-set, developing and enhancing it. Positive thinking is tremendously powerful and will ensure you're in the right zone for success in your sales career. Your whole thought process will be replaced for the better. Your client relationships will strengthen, and your confidence will grow.

There have been many case studies worldwide on the amazing effects of positive thinking. Lives have been dramatically changed for the better with health and wealth taking tremendous turn-arounds. All you need to do is simply browse the Internet, where there are hundreds of testimonies.

The way we perceive is the key to positive thinking. How you look at negative situations will directly affect your positivity. For example, do you consider a bad situation a problem? Or a solvable situation that will result in opportunity?

Positive thinkers do not ignore reality. They do not ignore negative events and bury their head in the sand. They instead look for the best in a situation, accept it, and look for ways to make things positive and create opportunities.

I had the pleasure of working with a person that never used the word "problem." He always referred to those situations as a "challenge."

If you have had a negative view on situations for some time, then you will have formed a habit. In every event, it's easier to find a negative or cast blame. Your outlook on life and cynical perception is now second nature. It has changed nothing and never will.

Time to change! Have some personal commitment and self-belief. It is easier to replace a habit than break an existing one. You have to focus on doing something new rather than concentrating on the thing you're trying to stop doing.

Here's a few tips that will help you become a positive thinker. Replace negative words with positive words in your everyday life. For example, replace your choice of words—"problem" with "challenge," "objection" with "opportunity." Be conscious of what you are thinking.

When a situation arises, and you automatically think of the negative, stop yourself. Asses the facts. Is it fear and assumption producing that thought? Look for the positive; there is a solution and an angle for opportunity. Look for it in every situation. Tell close friends of your intention to be positive; intent is very powerful. They are likely to pick you up on it if you slip up.

Never *react* to a situation; reacting is instantaneous without real thought and rarely has a positive outcome. Instead, *respond*. Responding means you have paused for reflection. This way you give yourself a moment to assess and understand the situation better. It allows you to digest the facts and challenges in front of you and gives you control to find the solution and opportunities. Better to have responded than reacted.

Try skipping the morning and evening news. Listen to upbeat music on your way to work. Carry a photo of something that reminds you of good times. When you are in bed at night, think of the positive things that have happened during your day, and think of the positive things and opportunities that tomorrow can bring.

Always set goals. Have daily goals, monthly goals, and yearly goals. Do not make them too tough. Achieving a goal, no matter how small, is a positive. Congratulate and reward yourself when you have achieved it.

Positive thinking will become a habit and be second nature with practice. Like the mind-set, it will not happen overnight. Once you have mastered the mind-set and become a positive thinker, you will become aware of dramatic changes in your perception of everyday life. In our case, you will notice a tremendous change in your approach to sales and your prospects.

You will find prospects warm to you quicker. They will want to spend more time with you and build a better relationship. They will bounce off your presence. Any positive change in a client is a good one, right?

Practice until it becomes habit. Many opportunities are out there. It takes a positive perception to see them. With enough practice, positive thinking will become habit, and it will seem perfectly natural to think positively. Negativity will no longer become the easy choice.

In creating the perfect positive mental attitude, the third and final stage is enthusiasm

ENTHUSIASM

Enthusiasm is taken from the Greek word *enthuse*, meaning "an inward God."

There is nothing more contagious than an enthusiastic and passionate person.

Enthusiasm is a visual expression. If you have mastered the mindset and positive thinking, it is nearly impossible to hide your enthusiasm. Enthusiasm is projected through your body language, the way you walk, the way you smile, the way you present yourself, the passion in your voice when you talk, and the confidence you radiate.

Even though it is an outward expression, enthusiasm is created from the inside. You cannot easily fake enthusiasm, or if you can, it does not last long. Think about the feeling you have the night before a holiday, the internal excitement it creates. The energy from that excitement must channel somewhere, which it does, as an outward expression. Even if you're not aware of it, you become visually enthusiastic.

If you like sports, think about the time your team was in a losing situation, then slowly started to gain control of the game, and started to fight back. Think about the enthusiasm you felt when you willed them to win. You are physically expressing your passion and excitement as enthusiasm.

The spring in your step is natural, the smile on your face is not fake, your presence cannot be missed, and your air of self-confidence is real.

So, how do we achieve and maintain this enthusiasm? Let's start with the feel-good factor. Feel good about yourself. Feel good about the inner change you are making. Feel good about finally ditching the negative views. Feel good about your positive outlook on any situation. Feel good about your future. Get passionate about it. Feel the excitement right down to your stomach.

Another great way is to book a great restaurant ten days in advance or book a weekend away a month in advance. Look forward to it. It will produce enthusiasm. The way you feel about it will show to others in a physical sense. Your voice intonation, gestures, and facial expressions can be infused with enthusiasm. There's nothing more boring than a monotone voice with little or zero gestures.

It's a challenge to maintain your enthusiasm to a strong level all the time; it does need recharging. If you find yourself slipping, increase the volume of your positive thinking. If you have a challenge in your day, remember to respond to it, then find the positive and potential opportunity.

People may be instructed by reason, but they are inspired by passion. To end on enthusiasm, here are a couple of quotes from great enthusiasts.

"Success is going from failure to failure without losing your enthusiasm."—Abraham Lincoln

"A person can achieve anything for which they have unlimited enthusiasm"—Charles N. Schwab

"One person with passion is better that ten people merely interested"—E. M. Forster

"If you're not fired with enthusiasm you will be fired with enthusiasm"—Vince Lombardi

A great attitude should become a way of life for any serious professional consultant. The three traits to a great attitude are mind-set, positive thinking, and enthusiasm, and they all require practice. Remember, the more you practice, the more of a habit you form. Once your attitude becomes habit, you will set a rock-solid foundation and pave the way to become a dynamic professional consultant that ensures your client will be influenced and focused on what you say.

You must take control of your mental approach; optimism is not enough. I noticed a fabulous poster displaying a sailing ship on the ocean with the words: "A pessimist blames the wind; an optimist expects the wind to change...A Leader adjusts the sails." Be the leader, and make the change in your attitude; it will not happen by itself.

We are human, and it's natural to feel different states of emotion. There is absolutely nobody else who can choose your attitude at any given moment other than yourself.

PROFESSIONALISM

"When your image improves, your performance improves."—Zig Ziglar

Professionalism is the difference between an occasional sale and selling with consistency. It is the distinct difference between average and great.

Throughout this book, I refer to you as a professional consultant, as that is exactly what you should be and constantly striving to improve. Professionalism is not something that should only be used in sales, but it should be a part of who you are and used in everyday life in everything you do.

"We are what we repeatedly do. Excellence then is not an act but a habit."—Aristotle

That's exactly what professionalism is—excellence. It's not what you do, it's how you do it that counts, especially in sales. People form opinions about you within ten seconds of meeting you. In sales, it is essential to set the right impression immediately. So, how do we attain the profile of a professional? The first step is self-professionalism. Self-professionalism is respect for yourself and your appearance. Your visual profile is vital, as it is the first impression you give to your prospect about your character.

Let's say it's late at night, and you are walking home from a restaurant, and across the road, you see a person, alone, wearing a hood, hands in his pockets. There's no one else around. How do you feel? Uneasy? Why? It's because you've assumed he's there to potentially harm you and obviously up to no good! That's because of his appearance, and you've formed an opinion of him in seconds. How would you have felt if it had been a couple, nicely dressed, walking a dog? They've probably been out, too, perhaps to the same restaurant as you. You don't feel threatened. Why? It's because their appearance is nonthreatening, and your opinion has reassured you that all is fine.

This works exactly the same way in sales. Your prospect will form an opinion of you on your appearance. He or she will initially trust you or not. Whatever sales line you are in, you must create the right appearance. Self-professionalism starts with health, hygiene, and grooming.

Many motivational gurus suggest a healthy, fit person is a productive one. Diet strategists promote exercise as part of a healthy lifestyle. People with addictions can be introduced to exercise to counteract or distract the craving. Whatever way we look at this, experts suggest exercise is good for the well-being of the physical and the mental.

This does not mean you have to be super fit and in contention for the next Olympic Games. A simple exercise regime, whether a regular brisk walk or similar, is a good start. Join a gym; paying for something normally motivates you to do it. Always consult a doctor or a professional before embarking on it!

"The mood-food connection is an everyday experience for most people, one that can be positive or negative."—Michael Van Straten, Good Mood Food

Watch what you eat! A healthy, balanced diet should be a lifestyle. Experts tell us different foods can create different moods. Some foods can make you feel lethargic, while others can boost your energy levels. Take time out to look into this. Research different food types on Internet search engines, and ask your local doctor or dietician for advice. There are many books available on nutrition and lifestyle. Morning and daytime television include nutrition and healthy lifestyle segments constantly. There are magazines dedicated to health and fitness. There's a wealth of information out there to help you achieve your goals for a healthy lifestyle. Help your body help itself.

The next step is basic personal hygiene. I once worked with a man who had an underarm problem. He permanently had two damp patches on his shirt in full view under his armpits. Clients would notice and avoid getting close to him. They concentrated more on his armpits than his pitch. Pick a neutral deodorant. Replacing a smell can be as bad as the body odor itself. When you smell of a musk factory, your prospects will either be revolted by the whiff or assume you wear it because you have a serious odor problem. Not good!

Don't wear aftershave or overdo the perfume; this is not a nightclub. Your essence of passion will not clinch the sale. You'll probably come across as "that salesperson with the cheap smell." Your powers of persuasion will be overpowered by your "splash it all over" indulgence. This is a distraction your prospects don't need. Keep them focused on you.

Personal grooming is your visual appearance. Use whitening toothpaste if you smoke or drink coffee. If you have been smoking or drinking coffee for some time, go to a dentist, and get your teeth professionally cleaned and whitened. There's nothing more off-putting than a beam of yellow when you smile. Invest in yourself; you will come up with the returns.

Take care of your hands; keep your nails trimmed, clean, and unchewed. Use hand cream to keep your skin supple and moisturized. Remember, you will be presenting your hands to your prospects as a greeting gesture and a sign of sincerity—your handshake. Do you think it sets the right impression if you present them with chewed nails and dry, sore hands to shake? How would you feel? Go get a manicure—yes, even the guys. A professional manicurist will not be shocked to see a man walk in. The manicurist will help keep your hands in tip-top condition.

Take special care of your face; it's what your prospects will be looking at the most. Let's start at the top to begin with. Keep your hair tidy and in control. Guys, keep it trimmed; you're a professional, and looking like a '60s rocker will not portray the professional image you need. Keep it sensible, with no piercings on display. Look after the skin on your face. Women are usually good at this! Guys, it's not a crime to use a moisturizer; flaky, dry, or oily skin is a put-off. Many of the major designers now have their own skin care range purely for men. Use under-eye serum; it will reduce puffiness and any dark circles. Looking like you've been partying until five in the morning is not recommended, as it makes you look as though you prefer to spend your commission recklessly and can lead to a trust issue. Women, be sensible with the makeup; don't use a trowel or look like an orange. Guys, if you must have a beard or a moustache, keep it neat and under control. Your best Dali impression will not be appreciated and is a real distraction to your prospects. It has been suggested that facial hair is not good in sales, and it can be perceived that you're hiding behind something, using it as a barrier between you and your prospects.

Dress for success! Make sure what you are wearing is appropriate and projects exactly what you are—a dynamic professional. Depending on the sales environment in which you are working or wish to work, dress smart. If you are in real estate, timeshare, door-to-door, or any other white-collar sales profession, it's essential to look the part. I worked in timeshare for a few years, and some salespeople dressed casually, wearing chinos and polo shirts as their attire, and some did pretty well. All the top, high-earning performers looked sharp all day, every day, wearing at least a shirt and tie. Some of the casual attire crew insisted they were selling holidays in a casual, informal arena. They preferred to project this casual image as they didn't want to appear under the bank-manager banner. What they projected is what they achieved. Many prospects saw them as tour guides, simply there to show them around the resort. A person there for a summer job. At the pricing stage of the presentation, they were not taken seriously enough. That resulted in a difficult close.

Think about it: let's say you have two timeshare salespeople in front of you, and it's the first time you meet them. You haven't spoken to them, and it's all about first impressions—image. One is dressed the casual way, and the other in smart business attire. You have $30,000 to spend on a timeshare; would your first impression sway you to give it to the sales person wearing chinos and polo shirt or the smartly dressed professional? The big difference is that casual attire projects a casual attitude, whereas smart attire projects a seriously dedicated professional who projects confidence. Be as sharply dressed as you can. That doesn't mean you need to go out and buy an expensive designer suit, but again, invest in yourself and your appearance.

First impressions will either create confidence or caution in your prospects. It is critical that you start off on the right foot.

The prospects probably know the pitfalls of your product and the not-so-good testimonials of past purchasers. You need to be the consultant, a professional who will reassure and reestablish confidence in what you have to offer. I know this is basic, but remember, you are having prospects forming opinions of you, and quickly. Don't give them a chance to form a bad one based on your appearance.

Finally, when you are just about to go through the door and head to work, stop! Take a good look at yourself in a full-length mirror. Would you buy from the person looking back at you? Does that person reflect professionalism? Enough for you to give him or her a chance to pitch without forming an immediate tainted impression?

TIME MANAGEMENT

Have you ever put things off? Important tasks, appointments? Most people have during their lifetime, but some people get into the habit of doing it. Most people put things off because they can't be bothered at the moment, and the task may be too difficult, or perhaps it's boring, and they prefer to be doing something more enjoyable.

Whenever you procrastinate, you are putting off important tasks and doing something else instead. Some people don't know they are procrastinating. They may think they are doing something that is urgent, but really there are more important issues to deal with before the task they are working on. They don't know how to prioritize the urgent tasks from the nonessential tasks.

Fear of being unable to complete the task is another reason they put off the challenge, especially important tasks. They hope it will all go away on its own and choose to do something they know they can handle instead. The problem is that it seldom goes away, and it usually comes back twice as big.

Tasks that don't get solved remain and form a backlog. New tasks add to them. There comes a point when you simply don't have the time to perform all the accumulated tasks. An angry prospect that you have to reschedule because of your inefficient task management has resulted in unorganized time management. That has had a knock-on effect on your next appointment that you will either have to reappoint or not give the time deserved. Then you realize the order you should have made last Wednesday, you forgot all about because you were so busy reappointing; how stressful is that?

Good time management is easy to achieve. Computers are in every household and every mobile phone has a calendar that is programmable for reminders. If you own a smartphone and have bad time management, then shame on you, because there are some great apps out there. Today, there are no excuses for not being able to organize yourself.

The Pareto principle, commonly known as the 80/20 law/rule states that 20 percent of something is usually responsible for 80 percent of the results. Pareto, an Italian economist in 1906, concluded that 80 percent of the wealth in Italy was owned by 20 percent of the population, and this is where the phrase began.

This 80/20 ratio soon became apparent in other areas of life. For example, 80 percent of the warehouse is taken up by 20 percent of the stock, or 20 percent of the sales team generates 80 percent of a company's volume, and so on.

The lesson in this case to us is that 80 percent of unfocused effort or being busy will only generate 20 percent of your goals. On the other hand, 80 percent of your goals could have been achieved with only 20 percent of the effort by simply focusing on the tasks that matter.

The important factor of time management is to ensure you concentrate as much of your time and energy on the relevant tasks—the 20 percent. The number of times I have seen salespeople with unorganized appointment books, frantically flicking through the date pages, mobile phone wedged between their ear and shoulder, trying to get to next week's page, usually with a pen that doesn't work, engraving the page by scoring into it with a dry pen, are countless. I have seen business cards falling out of their appointment book with scribbled dates and times on the reverse, only displaying their bad time management skills. Important appointments missed, tasks that have been overlooked, pressure from management, peers demanding to know why they are so behind schedule, and that overwhelmed feeling as a deadlines approaches. These are all examples of poor time management skills.

So, how do you avoid the stress of not having enough time? What can you do to ensure you arrive at the allocated appointment with enough time to prepare? How can you take control of your workload and organize it efficiently?

The answer is to have an efficient to-do list and the right approach to scheduling. A to-do list is very simple but can be extremely effective for organizing your day, week, or month and taking the pressure off. Make sure you only have one list. Don't have one for your personal life and another for business; one file is easier to manage.

A to-do list is a list of everything you need to do for that day and week. To maximize its effectiveness, you need to prioritize the list. First, make a list of everything you need to do for the week; look at the list in detail, and think of the consequences of each one, if you don't accomplish it within the week. Certain tasks will need to be done on a particular day, so pencil the date beside these tasks. The second stage is to distribute the tasks to the rest or your week with priority labels.

To prioritize, go through each one and put *HIGH* next to those that are of paramount importance and vital to be completed in that week. Write *MEDIUM* next to those tasks that are important but can be put on the back burner until the *HIGH* list is done. Finally, mark *LOW* next to those tasks that can wait and have the least consequences if they don't get done.

The trick here is not to have a whole list of *HIGH*s; if you do, take another look at them and reprioritize the less important ones. Once you have your list, mark a number next to each of the *HIGHS*s to prioritize them. *HIGH 1* should be the most important task on the list, *HIGH 2* would be done after *HIGH 1*, and so on. Once you have done this, rewrite your to-do list, starting with *HIGH 1* at the top, running down to the bottom *LOW* task. A priority ladder has formed.

You will now have a plan for your challenges for the week and an order in which to tackle them. You will not overlook or forget tasks, and you will not get stressed by the large number of less important jobs.

The next step is to create a schedule. This is looking at the time available to you and planning how you are going to use it. Invest in an appointment book, whether it is a book or an app. Make sure it shows hours in the day, days in the week, weeks in the month, and months in the year. This is the tool for your schedule. A good schedule will allow you to see what you can achieve with your time. It will allow you to make the best use of the time available to you.

Your to-do list and schedule should always be together. Transfer your to-do list to your schedule before your week begins, distributing your *HIGHs*, *MEDIUMs*, and *LOWs* throughout each day and in order for the week.

If you have a large task, it may be a good idea to break it down into smaller tasks. You can schedule these smaller tasks for quieter times in the week. When you come to working on the big task, it will be that much easier and won't take up as much time on your schedule.

Block daily, weekly, monthly, and yearly events that are important when you know about them. As the days go by, you will see up-and-coming events, appointments, or tasks that will allow you to schedule your to-do list around them.

When making an entry to your schedule, allow time for it, and allow time on either side. A task, meeting, etc., may take longer or shorter than planned. You must always schedule gaps in your day; this is very important for incidentals that occur. You will find that when the incidentals do occur, you are not stressed because you have time that you managed. Schedule breaks, and don't leave them for gaps; we all need break time during the day. Think about the task at hand; how long should it take? Am I relying on someone else? Do I have to travel to do it? Can it be done in one go? Think of all the components that are required to accomplish the task, and allow the time in your schedule to do it. Make sure you enter all the actions you must take to do a good job.

Interruptions can and will happen, but even interruptions can be prioritized. A client who telephones you unexpectedly, or a prospect who walks in the door is a high priority, but a colleague who is bored and just wanting a chat is not. The gaps you have in your schedule will allow you flexibility to move your tasks and reappoint if needed. That unexpected client on the phone or your walk-in prospect took up significant time, but you can still reappoint the day with correct time management, as you left yourself some gaps for such instances. Don't get into the habit of shifting your day around because you were too polite to tell your colleague you are rather busy. If he or she really needs to chat, meet up after work! If your scheduled break is interrupted by a high priority incidental, move your break to a gap. Doesn't this sound more professional, more organized, and more efficient?

Think, is a task really that vital, can it be a *MEDIUM*, or can you delegate it to someone else? The more you can delegate, the more free space you will have in your schedule. Follow up on delegated tasks and update your schedule with its progress until completion. Remember those *LOW*s? When you find yourself with a gap in the day that you left for those incidentals, and it hasn't been used, slot a couple in that you may have scheduled for later in the week. You will find those decreasing without realizing it.

The working day can change from day to day, and a *HIGH*, *MEDIUM* or *LOW* may introduce itself during the day. You have gaps and you have *LOW*s, so move a couple of *LOW*s to another slot in the week to make room. It's all about maximizing your time to accomplish tasks that are prioritized effectively and efficiently.

Keeping an efficient and organized to-do list and schedule requires commitment and discipline. You need to do this, and stay on top of it. Write things down immediately. Don't think, "I'll remember to put that in my schedule later." You will forget some of them.

Your schedule should be up to date constantly. Remember, repetition forms habit. Make your schedule a habit. Praise yourself once you have done a task. Cross it out of your schedule, and feel pleased that the daunting, stressful task is no more. When you meet your prospect, let them be the one who expresses, "Sorry, I'm late." You'll have the psychological upper hand in the meeting, and it will boost your confidence.

ATTITUDE

On a final note, now you are organized, so when you meet your prospect, check your attitude.

Professionalism in your attitude is fundamental. Prospects will pick up on your attitude easily. You can either choose to remain in a bad mood all day, blaming everything and everyone around you for your lousy day, or, alternatively, you can choose to switch your mentality, and change your mood to give out positive vibes. No one can do this for you.

It's your choice, and if you chose to remain in the lousy mood, it will affect your sales approach for the day. The real reason there were no sales was that the prospects picked up on your mood, and it affected their purchase decision.

Be positive, change yourself and your mind-set. Sure, we all have those trying times, but it's up to us to deal with it and move on. A sales professional who is upbeat, positive, and has great enthusiasm is very contagious.

To win in sales, you need a winning mentality. Winners have one thing in common—a great attitude all the time.

MAKE A FRIEND, LEARN THE LINGO, MAKE THE SALE!

We have looked at the accessible sources of information (the Internet) readily available to the modern prospect giving them insight into the pros and cons of your product or service. Today's client requires a more transparent sales technique to gain his or her trust and confidence. Even to these modern consumers, some of the old, tried, and tested sales tips are still as effective today as they were yesterday.

Making a friend still rates in my book as initially the most solid foundation for any sale to be built. Prospect rapport and finding common ground is the first step that any professional consultant should be actively trying to achieve. However, making a friend by itself will not make the sale; it needs to go a lot deeper than that.

Relationships create sales. The first sale that is made is you. If your prospects don't buy you, then there's no chance they'll buy what you're selling. Remember, the prospects will be extremely wary when you first meet, meaning their resistance and skepticism of you and your product will be at its strongest.

In most cases, they are more nervous than you, hence the resistance. After all, they are expecting a high-pressured, now or never experience. If your prospects have had time to prepare before you meet, for sure they've already made up a pact or excuse as to why they are not going to buy. Their pact can only be dismantled once you've been accepted into their circle of trust. Access to this *members only* club needs to be earned, and you must demonstrate your worthiness to gain entry. Friendly chat alone will not do. Every prospect you meet will be different, and you need to adapt accordingly to pass their test and be accepted as one of them.

Many salespeople assume making a friend is all about idle, non-business-related chit chat with the odd compliment being thrown in for good measure. Many find it a chore, hearing about the prospect's new grandchild or other mind-numbingly boring topic they've decided to land them with. "I've heard it a thousand times before!" is usually screaming through the salesperson's thoughts, while on the exterior is a perfectly practiced, insincere smile.

More often than not, the average salesperson will be so impatient to deliver the pitch that he or she will cut out the making-the-friend bit and replace it with a quick five-minute chit chat about the weather or something else that will fail to gain any trust or confidence from the prospect in the initial stages.

If you are working in sales now, how many times have you walked away from a non-buying prospect and thought, "I just didn't get along with him" or "They were really weird people" or "They were really cold, and I just couldn't get them excited?" The latter excuse, in most cases, is true, although it wasn't down to the product or the affordability; it was really down to the prospects' feelings. "We don't understand the salesperson."

If we look deeper into that last comment, it was because you were not talking their language. As you weren't communicating their language, they didn't understand you or want to understand you. I will elaborate on the importance of this a little later in this chapter.

Most sales trainers, especially in the corporate world, preach the importance of making a friend before entering into the sales pitch. They normally try to make the point that it creates trust and therefore makes the prospects more responsive and feel more comfortable with you as a person and not as a commission-driven monster out for their wallet. Trainers talk about the importance of non-business talk during the initial dialogue with the prospect in a sort of warming-them-up-first strategy.

This is all very well and good, but does it really work? Does it really put the modern prospect at ease and make him or her trust you enough to part with his or her hard-earned cash? Think about it, we've all been on a train, plane, or bus and sat next to Mr. or Mrs. "I'm going to talk to you, no matter what." He or she will talk about friends, family, maybe a trip, and many other experiences. After twenty minutes of this painfully boring talk, do you trust this person? Would you part with your money if he or she suddenly tried to sell you something? The answer is probably no, and you're probably thinking of ways to move to a new seat or praying for the movie to start, so you can plug in your earphones and end the pain.

On the other hand, have you ever been in the same scenario and found someone you've never met before to be really interesting? There was something about him or her that just made you hit it off from the start. You may have swapped contact details and promised another reunion. The question again is, why do we get along with some strangers so well and not others? "Group Language" is a phrase that most reading this book might not be too familiar with, yet it is the key to great prospect rapport and trust building.

To make it simple, today's world is made up of thousands of groups, each speaking their own unique and individual language. If we take, for example, a group of surgeons chatting in a social environment, they'd be happy conversing and bonding about new procedures, their last patient, pros and cons of the latest medical journal, and other technical jargon that most of us would have difficulty understanding. It goes further; once these surgeons stopped talking shop and started everyday conversational chit chat, their understanding and enjoyment of each other would still continue. Most of us would find it difficult, not being surgeons, to be accepted in their social circle because we are from another group, the one of professional sales consultants.

Let's continue. These same surgeons are chatting in a social environment, and we introduce a landscaper to their party. Awkward, isn't it? The gardener is a professional within his own right but finding it incredibly difficult to bond with the surgeons, as he doesn't understand or speak their language, and he's from the group of landscapers, one that has its own language, different from the one being spoken by the surgeons.

Even though people can be from extreme ends of the professional ladder, they can belong to more than one group. In this social gathering, the landscaper has started a conversation with one of the surgeons about horse racing. Both are passionate about the topic, comparing past horses to the thoroughbreds of today, to the flat season prospects, and their trainers. They have just bonded and are now talking their own group language: the horse enthusiasts group. This is a language the rest of the surgeons don't care to understand. The landscaper and that surgeon will be able to converse in idle chit chat, without awkwardness or prejudice, as they have found a common language they both understand. There is trust, warmth, and an understanding between them that is sincere.

You've just picked up two books on how to better yourself in sales, on the back cover of one the author boasts, "I wrote this book because I'm the best sales performer ever, and in every field I've worked, I've been number one easily. I'm going to show you how to do it, and maybe one day you might be as good as me and nearly earn as much cash as I do!" The other book cover reads, "Isn't it frustrating watching prospects walk away as non-buyers when you knew they should have bought? There was one thing missing that would have made the sale, but you didn't know what it was. Do you wish you could close that little bit better than you are doing now but just keep falling short? This book will share the successful practice from some of the highest achieving sales professionals in the world. In this noncomplex, non-jargon, simple English publication, you'll develop your existing talent, improve your closing rate, and increase your income." Which book talks your group language? Which one would you buy?

Every prospect you meet talks his or her own group language, and you need to be able to understand and converse in it, fast. You need to find a group topic you can both relate to. This is the ideal scenario as bonding will happen rapidly, and so will the trust, sincerity, and confidence it brings. Maybe you're both born in the same area or lived in the same town at some point. Maybe your parents or relatives are from the same region. Perhaps you share the same interest in a hobby, pastime, or go to the same place on vacation. Be careful with sports, because finding out you support rival or opposing teams will definitely cause bonding problems as you are from an enemy group. If this happens, bite your tongue, and do not go there, ever.

The easiest way to start your group search is to mirror your prospects using their own body language and spoken communication. Listen to them carefully, seek out words or phrases they use frequently. It may be that they chose to use "sure thing" instead of "definitely" or "cool" instead of "good." Start using these words back to your prospect, and you'll find they'll begin to warm to you.

Observe their body language; do they fold their arms frequently or clasp their hands behind their back? Do they nod when you're talking or interject with words of agreement? Mirror this back to them, and demonstrate physically you are from the same group. When mirroring, do it respectfully and subtly. You should start to notice a difference in them when responding to your questions. They may start to elaborate more without much effort on your part. You'll probably see them relax in their body language.

Once you have hit the group connection with your prospects, it will be pretty obvious. You will feel like you've known them forever, and rapport will flow effortlessly. Furthermore, they may start to mirror your body language as your connection grows.

Once you've been accepted into a group, never abuse it. In sales, honesty, transparency, and integrity are paramount in our efforts to become professional consultants. Never abuse or disrespect a newly found group member. The consequences will be no future business from him or her, and the group pipeline of referrals you potentially had has now vanished.

Once you've been accepted as a group member, your nonrelated business questions to them such as FORM (Friends, Occupation, Recreation, Motivation) will be sincere and not appear as a cheap attempt to create a shallow friendship just for pitching purposes that day. When working as a professional sales consultant, pitching to a fellow group member, you'll be listened to intently, respected, believed, and your advice on what to buy will be followed.

Keep in contact with your group members, and once the sale is done, don't disappear. Follow up is more important than the sale. The frequency is dependent on the sales environment you work in. Let them know at the point of sale that you'll give them a call or revisit in a day or two. This will gain you even more credibility and trust.

Group language is more than simply finding common ground. It is the bonding, understanding, and respecting of your prospect. It is about demonstrating sincerity and the genuine gaining of a friend. Done correctly, you will have a prospect for life and a great source for repeat business through him or her and future business through his or her other group members. Should you switch careers and start sales in a different field, you'll already have a list of group contacts to start working with.

I repeat, the first sale that is made is *you*.

SMART SELLING

To become a top performer, the focus is really on working smart, not hard. Anyone can be a busy bee; in sales there are many executives who work long, hard hours to try to attain results that usually don't come to fruition. This working method produces an exhausted, disillusioned, and underperforming sales executive.

Don't make the mistake of assuming that smart selling is simply shortening your pitch or cutting out irrelevant corners to save time. Smart selling is not about shaving minutes off your presentation. I mentioned the Pareto principle in chapter four, and it is probably the best example of working smart.

Smart selling is about timing, knowing what to say, when to say it, when to listen, and keeping it upbeat and paced.

Understanding your product and prospect thoroughly will assist you in pinpointing the features and benefits to your potential purchaser. Being concise, informative, and relevant will eliminate an unnecessary boring pitch that will drive your prospects to sleep.

PERFECT PREPARATION PREVENTS POOR PERFORMANCE

Perfect preparation really starts with the company you are representing. You must know absolutely everything about it. Where it started, who started it, how many users there were then, compared to now. You must know its evolution from the beginning and where it's heading in the future.

Understand how it works, the inner mechanics, pros and cons, literally as much as is humanly possible to know. Practice in front of a mirror talking about your company's facts and figures, test your knowledge, and become comfortable and confident with your answers.

As a professional consultant, the prospect considers you the CEO and expects you to be every department of your organization, and you'd better be tip-top on your product knowledge; there are no excuses here. The prospects' confidence hugely leans on what you know. The answers you give to their questions will determine whether they are comfortable doing business with the company you represent or not. Know everything about your product or service. Find out how it works, exactly what it does and does not do, the benefits both major and minor, who uses it, when it was invented or started. You must know everything there is to know about your product or service. You're a professional, and it's up to you to find this information out. Don't rely on others to tell you! Prospects can spot waffling. Waffling your way out of a product knowledge question you can't answer is unprofessional and unacceptable.

Even the best of the best can be asked a product knowledge question they can't answer at some point, and there is nothing wrong so long as you don't try to guess the answer. Be professional when this situation arises. "I really don't know the answer to that, and I'm keen to find out for myself, too. Let me just make a quick call to get the facts." (Also, find out why the prospect asked that question, as there could be more to it than you first thought.)

This is perfectly acceptable once or twice in your presentation. If you need to call three, four, or more times to get simple product knowledge questions answered, you will be perceived as uninformed and unprofessional.

It will promote a lack of confidence from the prospect, and it makes for very awkward and embarrassing silences while you're on the telephone getting answers you should already know. Remember, you're a professional, not just a salesperson, so project that image with your immense knowledge of your company and your product.

PROSPECT KNOWLEDGE

People won't really care about your product or service until they know how much you care about them. You need to find out as much relevant information about your prospect as possible before your meeting. Being forewarned and informed about the person in front of you gives you the edge and demonstrates professionalism, as you took the time to research what his or her potential needs could be.

If you need to contact a prospect to make an appointment, there's nothing wrong in saying something like, "Before we meet, can I just ask a couple of quick questions so I bring the documentation/ material/information relevant for you?" This shows you have an interest in them and will leave the prospect feeling good about your attitude when he or she hangs up. Remember, first impressions count.

Should you have an appointment at a business or company, take time out to research them on Internet search engines prior to your meeting. Knowing some facts about them and their clients will score hugely on your credibility rating. You should not be naïve and think you're the only person they've contacted or met while looking for solutions. Be one step ahead of the previous salesperson, and know about the company you're going to visit. This can lead to more needs being discovered and produce further sales or upselling.

One of the biggest downfalls of many average sales professionals is that they are so intent and impatient to get to the close that they only present what their product can do and not what the product can do *for the prospect*. Those three last words make a big difference and will influence the purchase decision on whether they buy from you or shop around.

Understanding the prospects and their specific, individual needs is paramount in making your product irresistible to them. We can explain how something works once we know its inner mechanics, but that's not sufficient to make a sale. For example, let's imagine there is a kitchen salesperson talking to two potential clients in front of a cooker. "This part of the cooker is called the stove. You turn this dial here, and that ring there turns red and goes hot. You can adjust the temperature of the ring by turning the dial; turning it left makes the ring hotter, turning it right makes the ring cooler, and turning it all the way back turns it off." A great description of how an element works on a stove cooker, the question is, did that excite you enough to blast your hand in your pocket and pull your wallet out to buy it there and then? Of course not, because you probably had the words "so what?" or "and I knew that...?" running through your mind.

This is because the salesperson was only explaining what the product can *do* (the feature). Factually, this was correct, and perhaps he or she will get a sale or two, but by presenting this way, the salesperson will definitely miss out on several potential future sales. You must point out the obvious and attach a benefit to demonstrate its relevance to your prospects. This way it shows what the product will do *for them*.

Features and benefits are a sales technique that has been around for many years. FABs are a clear and easy way to personalize a product to your prospect. Let's take a look at an example:

This car does not require you to insert the key to start the engine. Simply having it with you will allow you to push this button, and off you go. (Feature).

Then add the benefit:

This means you do not need to fumble around in your bag or pockets to find your keys anymore! So long as they're somewhere on or around you, that's good enough! How good is that? (Benefit).

Whenever you give a feature, always finish it off with a benefit, no matter how obvious it may be.

Understanding your company alone will not achieve great sales; it will only give your prospects confidence in who they're dealing with. They need to be absorbed into the product and mentally see and feel themselves using it. The only way we can achieve this is to understand what they really need. To achieve this, we need to ask them relevant questions prior to us presenting our product.

Just asking simple questions is generally not enough; in most cases, it's important to dig deeper and discover where their real hot buttons lie. Once you understand their hot buttons, you can give a 100 percent personalized presentation with the confidence that the prospect will give you their full attention. We call this stage Total Prospect Understanding (TPU).

As sales professionals, we must strive every time to achieve TPU with every client we meet. Remember, a great sales professional considers themselves as much a consultant as a surgeon.

Prospects should be informed that you are there to help them and not just to sell them. "I'm not here to sell you just anything; I'm here to make sure you buy the right thing. If it's OK with you, I'm going to ask you just a few questions, so I know precisely what you're looking for, then I can show you exactly the right product for you."

It is important to let your prospects know you will be asking them some questions before doing so, otherwise they will feel as though they are being interrogated. The vast majority of prospects will consent to your request, as it is for their benefit and will be relieved they have found someone who cares.

Should you get an objection when informing them of your pending questions, clarify why you need to again. "It would be unprofessional of me not to take the time to find out your specific needs, and I would not be doing you a service simply going through the motions, then advising you to buy the wrong thing. It's important to me that you've bought correctly, at the right price, and are going to be happy with (whatever you're selling)." Optional extra: "The majority of our business is done by personal recommendation from existing happy clients, and that's the way we wish to continue." Good for getting referrals from them when they've bought.

Let's go back to the kitchen salesperson and demonstrate a good way to let the prospects know you are there to help them, and you'll be asking them questions.

"That's a great stove you're looking at and very popular. (introduce yourself politely.) We have others very similar to that with different functions, styles, and sizes for different requirements. Let me show you them, so you can compare for yourselves. If I can, let me ask you a couple of quick questions to assist me in showing you the ones that will be of interest to you and leave the ones out that won't."

GREAT QUESTIONING

"It's not what you say, it's how you say it." True; however, it is important to ask the right questions, the right way. The questions you ask are as important as the answers you give. To make sure TPU is achieved effectively, your questions need to be structured and have a direction. You need to be focused on how your product will benefit your customers, the potential objections that might arise during your pitch, how they have been managing in the past, and what they've been using.

It's best to start with their past experiences of similar products. Discovering their past will show you patterns they have previously adapted. Find out what worked for them and what didn't. Discover why it worked and what they liked about it. Find out why it didn't work and the reasons they are looking for a new solution. Ask them what would be the perfect solution for them. Remember, this is the time to be the consultant and be asking relevant questions. Gather all the information you need.

Only your prospects can show you the path you should follow to introduce them on how your product is the perfect solution. The past will tell you what sort of prospects they are, the sort of budget they have already spent, the quality they are used to, and most importantly, the challenges they've experienced. It gives a great foundation for you to start forming a mental framework on how your pitch should be presented, what should be included, and what should be highlighted.

You should know about your main competitors, how much they charge, what backup service they have, their good points and bad. Make sure you know how they compare to your product in the positive and the negative. Using search engines is a great way to do this, as you can check out forums to gain insight from past users or purchasers of your competition. This really helps should your prospects mention a competitor's name, having bought with them before. You'll know the potential pitfalls they may have experienced based on the opinions of others.

Here are a few of examples of how to explore their past:

"Just before we start, is it OK if I ask you a few questions to help me ensure I'm showing you the relevant (model, service, etc.?) (fine).

"Have you ever used or bought anything like this before in the past?"

"Why did you buy it? When did you buy it? How much did it cost? Did it live up to your expectations? Did you get any challenges from it? If you could turn back time, would you buy it again? If you could change anything about it, what would it be? What would be the perfect solution for you?"

Those sorts of questions are only examples of what you should be asking. Remember, they are designed to help you form a correct picture of your prospects. Make mental notes of any key challenges or good points they mention, as they will come into play later on.

Don't be afraid to ask potential time-bomb questions, as these are the ones that prospects might react to ("If you could turn back time, would you buy it again?" and "Did you get any challenges from it?"). You need to find out the challenges they have faced previously. Without challenges, you can't offer solutions, and without solutions, there will be no sale.

Questioning the past requires you to ask "open questions." These are questions that begin with who, what, where, when, or why. These questions need elaboration from your prospects when being answered, not a simple yes or no. This will make your prospects elaborate and perhaps mention something important to the buying decision for them.

Make sure you dig deeper on certain questions to help you discover their real hot buttons and perhaps those hidden objections. "So, you didn't like the way the windows closed? Why? What would have been a better way?" or "The taste of the diet shake wasn't to your liking? Why not? What would have you preferred?" or "Your favorite vacation was in Egypt? Why?" What was the difference? Once you have an understanding of their past, you need to find out the criteria that will make them more open to buying your product.

Everybody has a criteria when making buying decisions. Time is usually taken to make a list of what their preferred choices would be. For example, when looking for a home, consideration is taken into the ideal location—is it close to schools, work, hospitals, and road networks? Decisions are made to the ideal number of bedrooms, size of garden, cost, and number of bathrooms.

When buying a car, the same applies. Do we go for diesel or regular, hatchback or estate, SUV or sporty, etc. You can say the same about kitchens, double glazing, diet products, clothes, TVs, and virtually every consumer good or service available.

As professional consultants, we need to find out and understand our prospects' criteria relative to what we're selling. If done correctly, the prospects will tell you exactly what you need to do to make the sale. The way to do this is very simple; just ask the correct relevant questions.

Do not bore the prospects with irrelevant questions. If they express that they are looking for a four-door car, do not start presenting FABs of the two-door version. Keep the questions focused on what's important to them.

Not every professional consultant has the luxury of having potential prospects walk through the door voluntarily. In some cases, prospects are forced to sit through the presentation and get gifted for doing so. The timeshare industry or some financial service sectors are classic examples of this. Others have to go and seek their potential prospects, like door-to-door salespeople or referral-based industries (although, we all must seek out referrals, no matter what field of sales we work in.)

Let's look at two different introductions to finding out prospects' criteria for buying. First, we'll look at one for a salesperson who works in a kitchen shop and second for one who works in the timeshare industry.

This is a great way to start your criteria discovery. The wording is such that you are not asking them "if" they'd thought about what they're looking for, you are working with them, as if you know they've got criteria. "What color and style do you have in mind?" The majority of prospects will go with you when you word it this way, especially when you say it with comfort and confidence; however, you may still get the occasional, "Oh, we don't really know, we're just looking at the minute."

If the latter is the case, open them up, what do you have to lose? The sales job starts when the prospect says no, and "We're just looking" is a no. If you do nothing, they will say thanks and eventually walk out. Never say, "Oh, OK, I'm over here if you need any help."

Remember: never react, always respond. The truth is, they do have a criteria in mind. The fact that they walked into your shop shows they are considering a new kitchen and will have discussed recently what they're looking for. If they are shown something irresistible, and it's affordable, and they like the salesperson, there is a potential sale.

The main reason the "we're just looking" excuse comes up is generally because they fear you are going to give them a high-pressured now-or-never pitch. They may not like what you have in store or perhaps fear you may show them something a little over budget.

The take-away and third-party stories sales skills are best used in this situation.

"That's great you're just looking; it's good to compare, and thank you for coming in to take a look at what we have. Please look around, and in the meantime, let me get some brochures for you to take with you. Just to let you know, we have so much more than what's on display here—different colors, sizes, and styles. Can you just give me an idea, so I get the right brochures? Do you prefer lighter colors or darker, and do you like more contemporary or classic styles?"

Don't be pushy or in their face, and make sure it is said lightly, and your body language is as though you're about to walk away to get the brochures. Done correctly, they could start to talk.

Take-away stories are very useful when dealing with nervous prospects. It is a great technique that gives them an exit. It is the complete opposite of FABs. It is clearly stating that what you have to offer might not be for them. The fact that you are agreeing with the reluctance can win over your prospects and open dialogue. The take-away story in the above example is:

"That's great you're just looking, it's good to compare…"

This answer is probably not the one the prospects were expecting. The fact that they were not pushed or challenged with the comment made them feel more relaxed and comfortable with the representative.

Other examples of take-aways could be:

"This may not be for you…"

"What we have may not work for you…"

Take-away techniques work in a reverse-selling method. If you try to convince someone that something is for him or her, he or she may take a "no it isn't" attitude (people do not like to be sold to.) However, if you tell someone something is not for him or her, then he or she may take the "it might be for me" attitude.

Third-party stories are also extremely effective when explaining your product or its usage to a prospect. This sales technique is telling a testimony from a past purchaser. It should be relevant and have a conclusion.

"We had the same question last week from a couple that came in. They bought the (explain the product) because it (explain the reason and how it worked successfully.)

Use an either/or close when you are asking them for an idea of what they're looking for. This means you give them a choice of two answers. In the example above, it's "light or dark" and "contemporary or classic," as they must answer one or the other. Never use an open question at this early point, such as, "Can you give me an idea?" as this will make the situation more awkward. The key is to get them talking, as without dialogue, you'll never make the sale, as you simply don't know what or where their hot buttons are.

I get many questions from people working in the timeshare industry, and the repeated one is that their clients always need to think it over before making a purchase decision. I have worked in this industry and agree that usually those who need to think don't return and buy.

Clients who need to think it over are generally not sold on the idea. The correct questioning and clarifications throughout the presentation have not been effectively applied. This subject matter is a book that I'm currently working on!

Let's take a look at the incentivized presentation like the timeshare industry. Remembering here, a good relationship has already been built, and now the sales professional needs to find out the prospects' hot buttons.

"John and Mary, we've already established this is not your last holiday, and you will be spending money on future holidays. The best way to explain how the ownership works is for me to personalize or tailor-make it to your specific needs. This way you can see if it fits your travel requirements or not. I'm going to ask you a few simple questions about the way you holiday, so I get a good picture of what you like and actively look for when booking your vacations. You mentioned that normally you book online, so we'll start there. What are your five main criteria when searching on the Internet for your vacations?

(Start them, if need be.) For example, is quality important? location?" (They'll soon get the gist of what you're talking about.)

Let them talk, but make mental notes of their main criteria. It's vital to follow up using open questions. "Your favorite vacation was Egypt? Sounds fantastic, what made it special?"

I like to call this "goal-oriented questioning." Adding an open question to their response makes them elaborate and in turn reveals key hot buttons you can use later in your presentation to them.

Failing to follow up on their responses is a complete waste of time, as you'll learn nothing about your prospects. Let's take a look at how *not* to do it.

"So, what was your favorite vacation?" (Response is Egypt.) "What was your worst holiday?"

The sales executive has just lost a fantastic opportunity to dig a little deeper into the prospects' hot buttons.

Here's a much better way: "So, what was your favorite vacation?" (Egypt). "Wow! sounds fantastic, what made it extra special?" They respond with anniversary, scuba diving, took the grandchildren, spouse loves history or loves the beach, the markets were fantastic, etc.

Much more information has been revealed about the prospects, and this will be used later in the presentation when demonstrating how the ownership works. When presenting the various destinations of travel, the representative can now include hot-button phrases, like, "Amazing scuba diving here," "There are really exotic markets," "The beaches are incredible, white as white with a crystal-clear shore." This allows them to buy what you're offering, as you are showing them what the ownership does for them.

UNDERSTAND, THEN CLOSE THE QUESTIONING

Once you've asked the questions, make sure you summarize the answers. This clarifies to your prospects that you've listened and understood. Active listening is vital, and you'll gain trust from them as they'll realize you care. Remember to briefly summarize; don't repeat word for word what they've said, just the main points.

"I think that just about covers it, let me just run it by you to make sure I've understood correctly. You vacation twice a year, normally in July and Christmas. Just the four of you travel. You take short weekend breaks two or three times a year. You love the beach and water activities, also golf is important to John. There needs to be kids' activities and shops within walking distance. You'd love to go to Florida, and your budget is around 2000 per travel. Quality is important to you, as is spacious accommodation. Have I about covered it? Have I missed anything?"

Now is a great opportunity to gain a commitment from your prospects. You know their criteria and budget. "What I need to do today is fit your personal criteria; I must show you something that gives the flexibility to travel during your preferred dates, the space of accommodation, the quality you demand, the activities you seek, and within the budget you allow. So, if I match your criteria and perhaps exceed it, I'm looking at my newest owners today?"

You may get a shaky answer from them, and if you do, then continue with something light hearted, like, "That's the normal answer I get at this stage, Mary. As you've already told me, you're going to continue taking vacations and spend money in doing, so really it's just a choice of where you spend it. I now know what's important to you and your family and will do my best to show you value and flexibility. All I ask is just to keep an open mind and see if it's something you can use and is affordable; if it is, great, and if not, that's fine, too. Is that OK with you?" (Yes).

No matter what field of sales you work in, all your questions need closing. I find it better to use the word "clarifying" at this stage. Make sure you understand what your prospects are telling you, and demonstrate to them that you do. Use phrases like the following throughout your presentation:

"Just to clarify…"
"Just so I understand…"
"What you're telling me is…"

Never guess or pretend you know what they're talking about!

RELATIONSHIP STRENGTHENING

RELATIONSHIP STRENGTHENING DURING QUESTIONING

In chapters five and eight, we discovered the importance of re-lationships in sales. People buy you first, never forget that. The criteria questioning session is a great time to bond better with your prospects and develop your relationship with them. The way you respond to your prospects using your body language and orally will affect your relationship with them. Be sure it develops and strengthens by getting it right. Getting it wrong will undo all your hard work and result in no sale. Being empathic and sharing emo-tions is the key. Be sincere, relate, and appreciate the situations they describe to you.

When prospects are responding to a question, don't over talk them or try to finish their sentences. Allow them to elaborate, and use your body language to demonstrate you are listening (nod, lean forward). Make understanding sounds (*uh huh, right, yes*) that don't interfere with your prospect's flow.

Active listening is a sales skill that must be followed every time. When your customers are talking, do not sit and stare at them with a blank look. Active gestures and relevant nods encourage your prospects to continue talking, as your motions indicate you are listening to them.

When they are talking about challenging moments they have experienced, use sympathetic body language gestures (head tilt, gentle head shake with eye contact). Use empathic words that show you are on board with them and appreciating. Make the words short at two words maximum, so they continue. (No, that's awful, how frustrating). If they are describing great moments, use your body language appropriately (nod, smile, laugh), and be excited with them. Use exciting words to demonstrate you are feeling it, too (wow, great, fantastic). To really show you are in their group, once they have finished describing a situation, add a little bit on to it. Nothing that could be controversial but just a little finishing sentence that shows you have *really* listened and understood:

"Oh, Mary, that must have been so fantastic to see your grandchildren there, and it must have been a wonderful surprise; and to think, you had no idea!"

"It's not just the fact that the other windows let the draft in, the mold growing on the inside must have been dreadful."

Relationships make sales, and a little chit chat at the beginning of your meeting is not enough. Modern prospects are aware you need to be friendly, and it's a part of your profession they expect. Sincerity, though, is probably something they don't expect. So, many sales professionals are too quick and eager to go for the business, and they forget the main foundation of the process—making a friend!

Relationship building is not about talking hours and hours of irrelevant chit chat. It is again about working smart. It's about reading your prospect and knowing when you've done enough to move to the next step of the sales process. The development and strengthening of your relationship should be done throughout your presentation and not all in one go at one particular part of your pitch. Spending way too much time trying to build a solid relationship when you first meet your prospects is not good either; they'll be keen for you to get on with it.

It takes practice to know when you've built enough of a relationship on the initial meeting to know when it's good for you to start talking business. Every prospect is different. My best advice here is to read body language, and if you see a prospect start to fidget or glance at his or her watch, you are taking too long. Keep it paced, but don't rush.

HANDLING OBJECTIONS

As humans, we have a natural flare to be inquisitive and sometimes judgmental. Throughout our childhood, we were taught to be cautious and constantly aware. Lawyers are renowned for erring on the side of caution, and the media thrive on the bad decisions people have made. The closest to us, our loved ones, family members, and friends can sometimes be quick to pass judgment and advise. How many times have you heard a loved one say something like, "Why have you bought that?" or "Buying that car was a stupid decision, why on earth did you do that?" or "We didn't need more encyclopedias!" and the infamous "You don't want to do that!" Loved ones always appear to know best.

Objections and concerns are a natural part of life and happen every second of every day. People gain knowledge from questions and can make decisions from the answers they receive. Not fully understanding something can create doubt or caution. A half-answered question could lead us to filling in the blanks incorrectly and making a decision based on inaccurate information.

Every professional consultant will be faced with objections or concerns, usually on a daily basis. The biggest challenge to the average salesperson is that objections are to be feared, or worse, still ignored.

Some salespeople have perfected the art of avoiding objections. They can flawlessly sweep the objection to one side and eliminate the need to deal with them. They can effortlessly ignore them and create an instant distraction to continue with their memorized, mechanical presentation. The problem is, their art never seems to pay off, and they get the same result time after time—no sale.

Average salespeople give up at the prospect's first objection and prefer to think of it as the excuse not to buy. Rather than consider an objection as an opportunity, the average salesperson will hang his or her head, think negative thoughts, blame the prospect for obviously being difficult, and find a reason to quit the pitch. The conclusion of this situation is, again, no sale. The prospect is somewhat confused as to why his or her questions didn't get answered, and the salesperson is left disillusioned, negative, and deflated.

Some salespeople get offended when presented with an objection, as if the prospect doubts his or her credibility and product, even taking it personally. The average offended salesperson will try to blast the prospect with a snappy (often sarcastic) instant killer response to the objection in an attempt to obliterate it there and then. Not only that, he or she hopes it will cause enough shockwaves to stop the prospect from even daring to elaborate further in his or her concerned questioning. The outcome of this scenario, once again, is no sale. The prospects will leave feeling embarrassed or even humiliated, never to return or recommend.

Objections and concerns are a natural part of the sales process. When you are demonstrating or explaining a product, you will hopefully get questions, as your prospects try to understand the concept themselves. What is totally unnatural and should raise the alarm bell is if your prospects don't ask questions with objections or have any concerns at all.

Prospect objections are great and should be welcomed. This shows interest in you and your product. This shows prospects are listening and focused on what you're saying. Objections are merely interactions from prospects who feel something needs further explanation or clarification. They are demonstrating that they are not simply going through the motions without any interest. This is active interaction from them and should be received with enthusiasm; it is a positive, no matter what the objection subject.

As professional consultants, we should be encouraging our prospects to tell us their objections or concerns, and this is essential for success. If you reach the end of your presentation and have not revealed all the prospect's objections, the chances are that you will not get the sale.

The more challenging objections to deal with are the hidden ones. They are the ones the prospect is not willing to give you voluntarily. These hidden objections are probably the concerns that mean the most to the prospect. Revealing these objections and resolving them is the key to most sales. It is imperative you find these. Use open-ended questions (Who? What? When? Where? How?) when asking key questions; this will make the prospect give you a more detailed answer rather than a simple yes or no, and it may reveal hidden objections. Using these key open words will make the prospect expand his or her answer to an explanation. Check out his or her body language when you ask key questions and look for positive and negative body responses.

Learn how to layer questions to help you dig deeper into your prospects' thoughts. Layering questions is a great way to open up conversation and help reveal hidden objections and nonbuying pacts they may have made prior to meeting you. Layering is a very simple technique, and it is purely a series of questions, the first being an introduction to the topic you wish to talk about. The questions following that are dependent on the prospect's answers.

"Why" is the most important and the most powerful word you can use. This really does get you an insight to your prospects' needs and requirements, as they cannot answer it easily in one sentence. It's all very well and good to ask questions; however, make sure you find the reasons for their answer.

Test the prospects throughout your presentation. Make sure they are listening and understanding. A good statement to use is "Based on what I have just said, what are your thoughts?" This is particularly effective if you have just described a particularly tricky part of your presentation, whether that be because it's complex to understand, or it's a potential flaw in your product!

While they are answering, never interrupt them. Do not try to finish their sentence by talking over them; you could presume incorrectly, and you might cut off a piece of information critical to the buying decision or hidden objection. You will also appear as presumptuous and rude. The professional will keep good eye contact, listen actively by nodding, and use occasional interruptions of "Yes," "Uh huh," "Right," or other verbal lines to confirm active listening.

No solid sale will be achieved unless all the prospects' concerns and objections are answered completely. Usually prospects will tell you their objections or concerns as they arise. It's important you understand the question in its entirety and that the prospects know for sure you understand them. Once your prospects have told you their question, repeat it back to them nearly word for word. Clarify what you have just said is correct and that nothing was missed. This will demonstrate you are listening and genuinely interested in them and what they have to say.

Repeating an objection back word for word can sometimes resolve it there and then by the prospects themselves. When they hear their objection spoken back to them by someone else, it can make it sound trivial or irrelevant on reflection. In some cases, if you are pitching a couple, one of the partners may answer the objection to his or her partner for you.

Don't just jump in and answer an objection outright. You may have a preplanned answer because you've heard it so many times, but this is not necessarily the best way to go. Never take an objection at face value. Make your prospects elaborate on their objection by asking and questioning it, for example, "That's a good question, and I'm interested, why do you ask that?" it is also important you don't sound condescending or sarcastic. Thank your prospects for the question. By doing this technique, you will soon discover if there is more to the objection.

Remember, always question an objection before answering it to make sure you fully understand the reason behind the question. Depending on the sales field you work in, you may have the same objections arise on numerous occasions. These are referred to as "common objections."

A good idea is to write down a list of common objections and the complete answers to them. Practice the responses until you are comfortable and confident in reciting them. If you know you have a common objection, and there are no strings attached to it, go ahead and answer it using your practiced response. Once delivered, make sure your answer is totally satisfactory to them.

Make sure you reassure the prospects that their objection is not stupid or isolated. Let them know there are others who have had the same concern, and there is a solution. A great way to do this is with a technique called "Feel, Felt, Found." Here is an example: "That's a really good question. Thanks for letting me know you *feel* that way. Mr. Smith, a client of mine *felt* exactly the same way. He *found* that if he did it this way..." What you're doing is acknowledging the objection (Feel), you are letting him know his concern is not isolated (Felt), and offering a tested solution (Found).

Another great way is to use third-party stories. Use examples of clients who have found solutions. For example, "That's a good question. Robert, a client of mine lives way up on a hill that's normally very windy. We installed the aluminum frames for him, and that eliminated all the drafts and in the process cut the noise out by 90 percent." Once again, you are demonstrating that you have listened and understood. You have reassured the prospect that he or she is not isolated in his or her question, and there is a solution.

Put a positive into the clarification; it can bring the objection in to perspective. "So, from what you've seen so far, you love it and can see the great benefits ownership brings for you and your family. The only challenge you have is that the check-in day is a Saturday and not a Sunday?"

Once you have answered the objection, it is important you get feedback from the prospect that you have answered it fully, and he or she is satisfied with your response. Never go on unless you get 100-percent-positive feedback from your answer. You must give them an opportunity to open up again if you have not answered them totally. Use questions like, "Has that fully answered your question? Please let me know if there is anything else that I may have overlooked or not fully explained." Get confirmation that the prospect is good with your answer, then close it. "Great, I'm glad that made sense!" Always add a quick and final closing line.

Never go back to an objection once you have answered it successfully. When it is in bed, leave it there!

Always be sincere when dealing with objections. Voice intonation is very powerful when responding to objections. Americans are extremely good at this, as a rule. When they respond to a question or explain something, their voice intonation usually rises at the end of the sentence, as if to say, "Does this make sense to you?" Voice intonation can also project confidence and authority when needed.

Speak with enthusiasm when responding to an objection. Putting a spring in your voice will also put an air of confidence in your answer. Remember, objections should be welcomed; clients are looking to you for reassurance. A confident tone is essential when a prospect is seeking clarification.

In sales, we need objections, and how we handle them mentally is the difference between an average salesperson and a great professional. Think positively, and adjust your attitude to embrace them, as they are buying signals.

Remember, an objection is not a rejection. Think of it as your prospect's curiosity or his or her need for clarification. For you, it is an opportunity to demonstrate why your product is definitely for them.

Never react, always respond!

WHY BUY THIS?

Many sales executives struggle and fumble with ways on how to sell an over questioning or challenging prospect. They try to find different approaches by bombarding the client with questions, most of them irrelevant and appearing somewhat desperate.

We must appreciate the prospects' point of view; they are simply asking questions to clarify or have more understanding. Each prospect we see will have different mental needs that require satisfying before he or she will decide to buy.

This may come across as merely excuses on why our product or service is not for them. Prospects may even state that a competitor's offer is more suited or more beneficial to them. Defending our product to an over objectionable client will come across as a desperate attempt to push the sale. Shoving the benefits at them might sway them to think about it but probably not make the deal today, if ever. Showing desperation or weakness will nearly always produce the same outcome—no sale.

Our goal is to allow the prospects to buy. We must never react to any form of objection or statement from our prospects. Responding with open questions back to the client is the road to success.

There are many studies on neurology in sales about why different approaches work on different prospects. I'm not going there in this book, but I firmly believe as professionals, we can satisfy every prospect with open questioning. Done correctly, we can make them orally elaborate their specific needs and gain an insight of what's important to them and why. With this information, we can find the right approach in our responses to them.

If you're ever in a situation where you feel that the prospect is being particularly challenging, or you work in an environment where the prospect is obliged to be with you through a promotion, there is a great way to get an insight into him or her. Simply ask why he or she would buy your product. Here's an example of how to put this into action with the challenging prospect:

"I really appreciate your concerns and questions and will continue to answer them to the best of my ability. May I just ask you at this point, based on everything we've discussed so far, if you were going to buy (this product), why would you buy it?"

Or, perhaps, to the prospect that's obligated to be there:

"So far, I've shown you some of the benefits that our product has to offer, and based on what you've heard so far, if you were going to buy, why would you buy it?"

This question really puts the ball back in the prospect's court and is a huge open question. It makes him or her respond with a reason as to why he or she might buy at the end of your presentation. It gives you the direction you need to head with him or her to hit the right hot buttons. It's a question the prospect probably won't expect.

It's always good to follow up with a polite, "Why?" once he or she has responded; it could open up another path for you to pursue.

On the complete opposite, another great question that should be asked is if there's something about your product the prospect doesn't like. This is a direct open question that prompts the prospect to share objections with you. Questions like this should not be left to the end of your presentation. Leave yourself enough time to handle and answer this correctly. Another benefit of this question is that it clearly shows the major points you need to satisfy before any sale is made.

Try to avoid the old tie-down technique; this does not work well with the modern prospect. A tie-down is really an assumptive close that does not require the clients to respond. A nod or a gesture is usually enough from them to allow the sales executive to continue. You are, in essence, answering for your prospects. Here are a few of examples:

"I'm sure you both agree with that…"

"We both agree it's a better way…"

"You wouldn't bother doing that anyway, I'm sure…"

The problem with is that the prospect may not agree with you but is too polite to contradict. If this situation happens, you could lose credibility, as it appears his or her opinion doesn't count, and you're being condescending.

Tie-downs can also cut off any potential hidden objections that could have arisen should you have asked an open question instead. It also cuts off any positives the prospect could have shared.

The biggest negative of tie-down statements are that they stop dialogue. I never use them, as in my opinion, they are a lazy, ineffective close that could come back and bite you at the end of the presentation.

Once answers have been given to an open question, it's important to close it. Clarification of your understanding to the responses is usually enough. It's imperative you do this before moving on, otherwise, he or she will feel you've not listened to them.

A much more effective way to close, rather than using a tie-down, is allowing the prospect to seal the close him or herself. The way to do this is simply by asking a closed question, one that can only be answered with a "Yes" or a "No." Here are a couple of examples of this:

"So, John and Mary, can you see the benefit in doing it this way now?"

"Would you say this is a simpler and more effective solution?"

Your questions must be designed so that a response is expected from your prospects. This will make them commit, with an option to question you further if need be—great for finding those hidden objections.

The questions you ask must be of benefit to both you and your prospect. It is essential to find out once or twice during your pitch just how interested he or she seems. This is usually done with a "Big Test Close" (BTC) midway through your presentation. The BTC needs to create an air of tension to gain an honest answer from them. It also takes courage from the professional consultant to ask a BTC. If done correctly, you will either gain a buying commitment or a reason why the prospect is not yet convinced, showing you the redirection you need to take.

Here is an example of a BTC for a window sales professional:

"OK, John and Mary, let's just take a moment to see where you're at. You told me you like the style of the windows, right? (Yes). And also, you can see the benefit of how they significantly reduce the noise and the draft right? (Yes). You also mentioned that you feel comfortable with the brand I represent, right? (Yes). Well, I've still got some other great benefits to show you, but, based on what you've heard so far, if these windows are comfortably affordable, would you be happy to place an order with me today?"

The BTC should leave no gray areas; the prospect should either give you a straight, "Yes," or a wobbly attempt at an excuse to stall you someway, which means he or she is not yet convinced.

Don't be put off by a "We'll need to think about it" or any other excuse; it's sometimes just down to the affordability. If you've been professional, asked and layered completely, and he or she likes what you're offering, there is no problem with you questioning this need to think:

"Thank you for letting me know, and I fully appreciate your wishes to reflect on what we've spoken about so far. It's important that my explanation of all the benefits I've shared with you have made sense. Can I just ask, so I may clarify and perhaps assist, what would you need to think about or discuss?"

Always go back to your prospects in a professional manner to gain the commitment. Here is another of example of responding, should your prospects not reply positively:

"Thank you for that, John and Mary. Can I just ask again for my understanding? Do you like the windows? (Yes). And you can clearly see the benefit of the noise and wind reduction? (Yes). Or is it me, have I not done a good job and failed to show you the value of these windows? (The prospects will excel in how great you've been.) Or is it the initial down payment?" (This could be the real reason.) From there, you can move forward and close.

The usual reason that the prospects need to think about it normally comes down to the money side of things. Let's rewind a little. You do need to be certain it's the money that's stopping them from buying, and there's a sure way to find out: ABC (Always Be Closing).

ABC should be used throughout your presentation, and although extremely transparent and innocent, is hugely powerful when asking for the business at the end. If done correctly, it will almost guarantee the reason for not buying is down to the initial payment.

ABC is a step-by-step process to gain commitment from your prospects through a continual series of small closing questions. Your goal is to make them accept that they can use your product and appreciate its value. It also allows them to voice any concerns they may have.

The closing questions should be well timed and not appear forced or with stage fright. They should be spoken with comfort, confidence, and ease. Relationship building must continue, but you must know what your prospects are thinking at regular intervals. This gives you the direction you need to follow or change before you

Here are some examples:

"Can you use it (product)?"

"Does it make sense?"

"Can you see the benefit?"

"Can you see the value?"

ABC should also be mixed with open questions relating to your product's usage.

"How would you use it?"

"What would be your reason for buying this?"

"What benefits can you see to this?"

"Why would you not buy this?"

That last question is one that many average salespeople might be too fearful to ask. Remember, we need to find those hidden objections and cover them. The answer to this question will probably be the cost. If it's not, then the prospect will tell you what you need to overcome in order for him or her to say yes.

Many average sales executives talk far too much, not allowing the prospects to absorb for themselves the full benefits of the product and the reason for them to buy. In most cases, an over-talkative salesperson makes them switch off. Remember, there is nothing sweeter than the sound of the prospect's own voice; let them talk.

If you feel you are talking too much, you probably are. When you talk, you're selling. When the prospects talk, they're buying.

ABC and open questions are there to allow your prospects to buy what you're offering. You must actively listen to the answers and the reasons to those responses. Remember their answers, as you'll be reminding them of what they said at the end of your presentation. ABCs and OQs let you know exactly where your prospects are at and the direction you need to take. If you effectively execute ABC and OQs, you can easily overcome the "We need to think about it" objection at the end.

"Can I just clarify with you, John and Mary; you told me you can use it (give some examples of usage they told you) and that if it was comfortably affordable, you'd take it. Now I've showed you the price, you need to think about it. (Don't allow them to interrupt.) I'm here to help, especially with the payments. You've told me you love it, can use it, and want to take it, and I want to help. Tell me, what would be comfortably affordable to you?"

Quoting what they've said is the ultimate close and can confirm that the money is the real challenge.

Even though it's fine to challenge the prospects, it must be done with empathy, professionalism, and appreciation. Your objective is to promote and sell your goods, and at times, you may feel that your prospects have not been honest with you. Your attitude is always your choice, and if you react, no sale will ever be achieved.

As a final offering, if I have a prospect who has not bought, I will always clarify with them the definitive reason for not doing so. You may just get one last comment you can work with.

"Many thanks for coming to see me and taking the time and interest. I certainly have enjoyed our time together. Just as a parting clarification, the reason you are not buying today is because (then state his or her reason back to him or her.)

BASIC SALES SKILLS AND CLOSING TECHNIQUES

I n this chapter, we are going to look at some basic sales skills. Throughout this book, there are several examples of sales skills in motion, and some are repeated in this section. This is a good reference chapter for you to come back to and practice.

Although we have focused on the importance of being a professional consultant and the development of a great prospect relationship, it is still (probably more than ever) important to use sales skills when presenting your product.

The words "sales skills" can drive fear into most people's bones, as they consider them some sort of black magic or voodoo that tricks people into buying something they really don't want. What are sales skills, and why are they perceived in such a way?

It is fair to say that the perception of sales skills is that they are simply a line of lies told by some dodgy person to make a quick buck. I'm sure there are many people reading this book who may have been on the receiving end of that or may know someone who got ripped off. Well, lies and deceit are one thing, true sales skills are most certainly another.

Used correctly, sales skills are great for aiding the sales professional in describing the product and allows them to determine if the prospect understands and helps them reach a purchase decision.

Sales skills should be used throughout your presentation with transparency. They should flow with your pitch seamlessly, and there should be no tension when you deliver them. We use sales skills in everyday life, although we might not know we are even using them.

"Would you like tea or coffee?"

You can say that line without any nervousness, fear of repercussion, or losing a friend, yet, it is an either/or closing technique and hugely effective. You have made a pitch (tea or coffee) and only allowing the person to respond with one of two answers. You are not asking if the prospect would like a drink, you're telling him or her they're having one, and it's up to him or her which one to choose. There was no trickery, lies, or deceit. This is exactly how sales skills should appear when used correctly. No waffling, just relaxed, and to the point.

Sales skills are there for clarification, description, understanding, confirmation, and direction. They should let you know where your prospects are at, allowing you to change sales direction if need be for the benefit of both them and you. They are great for handling objections and directing "questioning" prospects to see a clearer picture of understanding.

Different sales skills will be used at different times throughout your presentation. Some will be quite light, for example, seeking some basic information from your prospects. Others will be more intense, like when you are going for the sale and gaining commitment.

Even though I mentioned there should be no tension from you when delivering sales skills, on occasion, it is necessary to create tension in a question to get a definitive answer from your prospect. Done with the right technique, it is extremely effective.

Some sales executives fear using sales skills, as they think it might somehow undermine the relationship they have formed with their prospects. It's not what you do, it's how you do it. Remember, you need to be constantly developing your relationship with your prospects. With that in mind, you can strengthen your bond using sales skills. Should a tense closing question be necessary, you lighten up the conversation immediately after answering (if need be).

Preferably, your relationship should be that strong with your prospects that only a personal insult should ruin any relationship you have with them. I've personally found that when I ask intense closing questions, my prospects respect me more, as I am asking in their best interests, and in most cases, simply pointing out the obvious. Some fear using sales skills, as they think it might sound cheesy. This will definitely be the case if you don't practice them, so you are comfortable and confident when using them.

The challenge is when a sales skill has not been practiced enough, and you appear to change personality when delivering them. Your smooth flow will suddenly hit air turbulence, and it will be obvious you are throwing in a sales technique. This will take points off your trust and confidence score.

You need to practice and perfect the delivery of your sales skills. They will then flow as naturally as you say your own name and birthdate. Once you get to this level of confidence, it will not sound cheesy, and you will come across as a solid professional consultant with transparency. No detection whatsoever of any sales technique will be made. You will get the answers you need, and the prospect will have the understanding he or she requires.

The other reason sales executives don't use sales skills is they fear the responses they may get from the prospects. They don't want to hear a negative response or an objection.

This is exactly what we need to hear from our prospects, either a positive answer or an objection. Both are a win for us. If it's a positive answer, then great, move on. If they object, that's just as good and shows they are listening and showing a level of interest. You've simply uncovered a concern or clarification issue from the prospect—well done! As in the earlier chapter, dig deeper to find out more using open questions, then go ahead and answer it. If the objection hadn't been revealed by the prospect during your presentation, then the probable result would be no deal.

Remember, people don't like to be sold to, they prefer to be allowed to buy. Sales skills are used for exactly that purpose. They are an aid that benefits both the prospect and yourself.

Listed below are some basic sales skills and their meanings, along with some different closing techniques you should be using. Adept them to your own personality, and practice them. Some you'll find you like and with practice get along with, while others might not fit your personality.

Remember, if you continue to do what you're doing now, you'll achieve the same results. Get out of your comfort zone, and try them!

THIRD-PARTY STORIES

Telling prospects of past client experiences is a great way to generate confidence. It is a great technique in handling objections, too. As young children growing up, story reading fascinated us, whether it was a teacher in class telling it or parents reading to us before going to sleep. We remained quiet and listened intently, absorbing all the information being told to us. This can have the same effect on our prospects. Simply tell your prospects of a similar client concern and how it was solved. No matter what the objection, comment, or praise from a prospect, third-party stories work.

"Actually, John, the last customer bought it for exactly the same reason you just mentioned, its portability."

"Funny you should mention that, Mary, because we had the Smiths buy exactly the same model two weeks ago with the same situation, and it worked perfectly."

EITHER/OR CLOSE

Only ever give prospects two choices, any more, and they'll need to think about it and probably not come back. We must do a thorough investigation into their needs, and make sure as professionals we are showing them the two options that are correct for them. Don't fluff around here, be direct and to the point.

"So, we can really bring it down to either the red or the green, which one would you like?"

"Great, would you like the wooden frame or the steel frame?"

FEEL, FELT, AND FOUND

One of the best ways to handle an objection. This can only really be used once during your presentation. It is a great technique to make prospects not feel isolated in their concern while demonstrating there is a solution. You orally use the words "feel," "felt," and "found," in that order. It's usually used in conjunction with third-party stories.

"I appreciate how you *feel*, John and Mary. A couple that purchased last week *felt* the same as you do, and they *found* that (give the solution.)"

PICTURING

Picturing is a great way to allow prospects to see themselves using what you're offering. It works tremendously well in sales where the prospect can't actually take home, use, or see results from his or her purchase immediately after the sale, such as real estate, timeshare, financial services, and dietary products. In these cases, picturing must be used throughout your presentation. It is important to be picturing relevant scenarios to your prospect based on the information he or she provided you with during your research questioning. The descriptive words you use and how you use them are imperative to the impact it has on them. Active words should replace mono (boring) words.

Picturing is different for every prospect. If I described the perfect car to a group of people, each would hold a different image in his or her mind. The words used must stimulate the main senses: smell, touch, sight, and sound.

"Beautiful" could replace "nice." "Fragrance" could replace "smell." "Fantastic" could replace "good."

"Imagine the aroma of roasting coffee coming from your new kitchen, Mary."

"Can you imagine the looks of delight on your grandchildren's faces when you tell them they're coming on vacation with you here next year? Can you see them splashing and having great fun in the pool with their new friends? Make sure you don't forget your camera!"

ASSUMPTIVE CLOSE

This is a strong technique that assumes your prospects are buying. The words you use do not question whether there is an *if* to the purchase decision. It is presented throughout your presentation but must be used carefully, as it may appear you are railroading them, and should they feel this, you could lose the sale. If used correctly, it is very effective.

"Great, will you be paying the deposit by credit card or cash?"

"We'll get that shipped to you by next Friday, can I take your address?"

FAB

A classic from yesteryear that is still as good today as it ever was. It stands for Features, Advantages, and Benefits, or to some, simply as Features And Benefits. This works in any field of sales and is very easy to use. It makes the difference between an information person and a sales professional. The "feature" points out the obvious, such as:

"There's the pool."
"This is the kitchen."
"There's the lock."

A feature alone is pointless, as most prospects would probably think it's obvious. You *must* back your feature up with an immediate benefit:

"That means you can take a cool, refreshing swim on a hot day like today."

"With easy access to the back garden, so you can enjoy those summer evenings dining outdoors with the family."

"That not only makes it secure but also means your children won't be able to access the main road outside."

A presentation without FAB will result in many potential buying prospects walking away. Use FAB all the time.

COMMITMENT CLOSE

This is a great closing technique for the haggling prospect. Should you have prospects that want something extra to make the purchase decision, make sure you gain a commitment from them first. Don't go making phone calls or wasting energy on prospects who just may be giving you the runaround. You may do a lot of unnecessary work and spend time calling people to authorize their demands, only to hear them say, "We need to go and think about it." Gain the commitment of the sale before you do any extra work.

"For me to include that, John, I need to make a phone call to get authorization, as I'm not permitted to do so. Before I do that, if we can go ahead and do what you're asking, you'll sign now, right?"

ONE, TWO, THREE CLOSE

A very effective way to get the sale at the end of your pitch. You give your prospects three reasons as to why they should go ahead and buy with you right now. The reasons should have been mentioned by your prospects earlier in your pitch, usually during your questioning. After each reason, pause and wait for agreement. Immediately after you've given them the third reason, and they've acknowledged, ask for the business.

"John and Mary, just to clarify, first, you like it, right? As you told me earlier, it has the space you need in the back to take both sets of golf clubs. You can use it, and it'll make your life easier. The grandchildren will have enough space back there, and you liked the small TV screens on the headrest to keep them quiet during those long journeys. And finally, the down payment is comfortably affordable, yes? (Yes). Great, congratulations (shake hands), you're going to love it, now let me get the order form..."

ABC ONE

Always Be Closing. Another sales skill that should be used all the time. Used correctly, ABC will be transparent and unnoticed by your prospects. I like to refer to it as short and simple clarification questions that only need a "Yes" or "No" answer. It is a great way to get feedback from your prospects that will determine if what you're saying makes sense to them and if they agree or disagree with you on a particular point. ABC gains several small commitments from your prospects throughout your presentation that can be used at the end to summarize the reasons why they should be buying. The first three examples below are ABC questions, and the fourth is an example of using the information you've gathered toward the end of the presentation.

"Is the space big enough for your golf clubs?" (Yes).

"Will the Grandchildren be comfortable in these rear seats?" (Yes).

"Will the parking sensors assist you with reverse parking? (Yes).

"Just to recap, John and Mary, you've told me the rear space will fit your golf clubs, and the backseats are comfortable for your grandchildren. Also, the sensors will certainly assist with parking at the grocery store." (Now, on to the close.) ABC must be used immediately after you've answered an objection to make sure you've completely covered it.

"Does that answer your question completely, and are you totally happy with that?"

EMPATHY CLOSE

Side with your prospects when they are telling you about a challenge they've had in the past. Be sincere, and try to appreciate their feelings during that time. Never interrupt, but demonstrate active listening and empathy. They will gain a sense of relating to you and so strengthen your relationship. Your suggestions will be much more acceptable, and closing an empathic friend is much easier. I must highlight again: be sincere.

"I can't believe that last company deserted you when your windows became a problem. The draft you're telling me about must have been unbearable, and the cost of your heating bill to compensate has been really expensive. Let's end this nightmare now. What I've shown you is the solution to the draft and the expensive bills. I'm here to help and going to assist in every way I can; is this down payment comfortably affordable?"

PENCIL PRO AND CON CLOSE

This classic is still as good today as it was years ago. This is generally used on prospects who are indecisive. It must be used at the end of your presentation and is a great way to allow prospects to buy in themselves. Take a piece of paper, and at the top of the page, write two words next to each other: "Pros," then "Cons." Give the piece of paper to your prospects, along with a pencil. Ask them to list all the reasons they should be buying what under pros. Then request they write down all the reasons they shouldn't be buying under the cons. Start them off under pros with a couple of examples you discovered during your smart questioning, and then leave them to it. Excuse yourself for five minutes, allowing them to continue.

This will allow your prospects to discuss alone the reasons it's a good idea to buy or give them time to come up with any last objections they wish to run by you. When you return, and if you've done a good job, the pros list will far outweigh the cons list. The close then is easy as they themselves have demonstrated to themselves why they should be buying.

"As you can see, John and Mary, with the list you have written yourselves, it makes perfect sense."

ABC TWO

Attract attention, Benefits, and Credentials. This sales skill is used when presenting to a group of people. It is extremely effective, and when used correctly, it will hold their attention for long enough to get all your points across.

The *A* stands for Attract attention. This *must* be the first thing the group hears you say. You should shout out a quick statement or comment that is loud, clear, and precise. It must command your group's attention immediately and shock them into silence. You now have control.

B stands for Benefits. This is where you tell your now silenced group what they are going to get out of listening to you. It should be a brief summary and to the point. Choose your words carefully, make them exciting, and descriptive, and that will make them want to listen.

C stands for Credentials. Your audience needs to know why they should be listening to you. Tell them of your great experience and expertise that demonstrates, without question, that you are the right person to be in front of them.

(*A*) "It's a great morning, welcome!"
(*B*) "Over the next twenty minutes, you are going to be inspired, invigorated, and..."
(*C*) "Let me start by introducing myself. I'm Colin, and I've been involved with..."

READJUST THE PACT

This is a skill that requires you to do nothing. In most cases, prospects have ready-made excuses as to why they are only with you for information, no matter what they are not buying. As you work through your presentation, their feelings should change if you are doing a good enough job as a professional consultant.

The only people who can change or readjust the pact are the prospects themselves. They will not do this in front of you, as they are too embarrassed to admit they had made an excuse before meeting you. Therefore, you must excuse yourself at least two or three times during your time with them, so they can talk privately. If you don't, then they will not know each other's thoughts, and this will result in a "We need to talk about it first."

Leaving prospects will allow them to ditch the pact and become more open minded. It could also be a good time for them to discuss concerns, especially if one of the partners is particularly quiet.

When you return, you'll either be greeted with smiles and a greater development with your relationship or faced with an objection. Either one is good; if it's an objection, it can be dealt with and closed. If it's smiles with a more relaxed body language, then continue the way you're heading.

NO LONGER A STRANGER

Make a polite excuse to leave your prospects for a couple of moments five minutes after meeting them for the very first time. If you have made a great first impression, when you return, you are no longer a stranger.

WHEN IN DOUBT, ASK, "WHY?"

"Why?" in sales is your biggest friend. If you are faced with a question that you don't know how to answer, or you're not too sure why the prospect asked it, don't guess on what he or she meant, simply ask why he or she asked.

If prospects are responding to one of your questions, and they answer with something totally different from what you were expecting, then asking why should again be included in your reply.

When making questions to prospects, asking why will provide the map you need to follow with your presentation. It will make them tell you what's important and what you need to show to hit their hot buttons.

"Why?" is a great open question, and it cannot be answered with a "Yes" or "No"; prospects must elaborate. If used a second time, it makes them elaborate even more, allowing you to dig deeper, perhaps revealing an objection, hot button, or a required change of direction.

As a professional consultant, we cannot fully recommend something without knowing the needs of our prospects and *why* it's important to them.

Finally, don't just reply, "Why?" First, thank them for asking the question.

"Many thanks for answering (or asking), that's a really interesting point. May I ask why you asked that?"

TALK LESS, SELL MORE

The more you talk, the tougher the sale, the more prospects talk, the easier the sale. As mentioned previously, the biggest crime any sales professional can commit is to talk way too much. Prospects will switch off, boredom will set in, and an excuse to leave will shortly follow. Your silence is one of your biggest assets. Allowing prospects to open up and converse is your key to gaining stronger client relationships. It will provide significant information about the kind of prospects in front of you and what's important to them. The easiest way to do this is by using two different sales skills—open questions and managed silence.

Open questions are ones that cannot be answered with a "Yes" or a "No." They must start with who, what, where, when, or why. Once you've asked an open question, back it up with another. Make sure you actively listen, and be involved with their answers. Dig deeper, if need be, but be careful not to make it sound like an interrogation. Keep your open questions light and to the point, and don't stray from your objective.

Never interrupt your prospects, and learn the art of managed silence. This is one of the toughest disciplines for any sales professional to master. You need to make the prospects talk, and getting them started is usually the most challenging bit. Once you've asked an open question, shut up! Remain like that until they've not only started talking but until they've finished. Sometimes it will feel like an eternity until the prospect starts to respond; it's not, it just feels like that.

Important tip: he who talks first, loses. If you start talking first after asking an open question, the prospect could consider you rude, as you didn't allow them to answer. Even though you thought the prospect wasn't going to answer, or you were too impatient or embarrassed to wait for his or her reply, the result is the same either way: he or she will close up from then on.

Remember, you probably don't know the people you're presenting to yet. You have no idea how reflective they are before they answer a question. Give them time to begin to answer your open question and the respect for them to finish answering before you talk again. If the prospect starts to talk first, he or she will start to gain confidence in responding and start to elaborate more freely with time, as he or she will begin to relax. You'll be rewarded in gaining knowledge of the sort of person you are presenting to and gather the hot-button information you require to make the sale. Don't forget to actively listen during your managed silences.

TAKE-AWAYS

It is always better to sell from a position of strength. Prospects can see desperation very easily, and this could deter them from purchasing. The easiest way to sell from strength is by "taking away" the product from them. It is simply you advising the prospect that your product or service might not be for him or her. Like with a child, if you take a toy or game away from him or her, her or she will want it more. This works in exactly the same way in sales.

When you take away your product, it instantly eliminates any trace of desperate selling in the eyes of the prospect. It makes them realize that your offering is that good, and you can somehow be selective who buys it. When you use take-aways, do it professionally and with politeness, never with a stern tone in your voice, as it might well be perceived with sarcasm.

Finally, it achieves our goal of presenting as a professional consultant, only concerned with the prospect's best interests, and this is projected in this sales skill.

"John and Mary, what I'm going to show you today might not be for you. I'm not here to sell you just anything, I'm here to make sure that if you like it, you're buying the right product."

WORDING

Choose the words you use carefully, as they will affect the outcome of your prospect's purchasing decision. You could innocently plant seeds of doubt in the minds of your clients that they will have grown later on in your presentation.

Try to eliminate entirely some evaluating words like "decision." This word automatically triggers our brain to consider, ponder, and evaluate. When these words are used to a prospect, it nearly always ends with a "We need to think about it." He or she now need to do so, as your word decision triggered a "need time to evaluate before deciding" thought.

Replace "decision" with "choice." Exactly the same meaning but much more flowing and easier on the brain's thought process. Asking a prospect to choose between one of two options can easily be done, and usually you get a choice from them right away. You are also giving an assumptive close with choice, as it means "which one?" unlike the word "decision," which represents, "Do you want it?"

Another word to replace is "think," as this also gives a reflective thought process. Asking prospects what they think usually tends to lead to the negative side of thought as human beings can easily err on the side of caution instead of looking at the positive.

"Make sense?" is a much better alternative. Making this statement with your voice intonation rising at the end of the word "sense" also makes it sound like a question. You normally get a positive response from these types of phrases.

There are many words that can influence the thought process of prospects, I could have dedicated this entire book to this subject alone. Just take some time and self-check your pitch carefully with the words you are using. Practice replacing them, and make your new words a habit.

BODY LANGUAGE

B ody language, or as I like to call it, the unspoken language that speaks volumes, claims that the majority of all communication is projected through our body and only minimally through the spoken word.

Body language is a physical communication that very few people are aware of. Every day, people are sending thousands of signals and expressions of their state and feelings, yet very few people notice them, or importantly, know what they mean.

Next time you're in a café, bar, or any other social environment, try people watching. Focus on a couple or a group, and look at the way they use their body while talking. Observe the touching of hair, the folding of arms, heads tilted at an angle while listening, the tapping of fingers on a bar, the crossing of legs while seated, the raised eyebrows, the clasping of hands, eyes rolling, the foot tapping, and so on.

There are hundreds of movements, and all of them are telling the person they're communicating with their feelings, whether that is "I'm bored" or "I'm really interested," or maybe in our case, "I'm close to buying" or "I'm lying."

Like attitude, you cannot hide body language. Your physical expressions happen naturally. Starting from the subconscious, your feelings are projected in a chain-like reaction, progressing until they are visual to the person or people you are communicating with. In sales, it is important we get familiar with certain types of body language and understand their interpretation. It is easy to be lied to when someone is speaking to you, but body language might just tell you something else a little closer to the truth.

Many potential prospects may tell you they understand what you are talking about and the benefits of your products, when in reality, they haven't got a clue and are too embarrassed to admit it. The thing here is not always to believe the spoken word when communicating with prospects. Always back up what they are saying at key moments by observing their body language. They will be so busily wrapped up with what they are saying that they will forget their body language is perhaps saying something to the contrary. Be sharp and observant.

Many prospects have their reasons to throw you off the trail. Maybe they're afraid they can't afford it, maybe they don't understand what you are pitching, or maybe they're afraid of sales closers. Whatever the reason, you need to know when they're not quite telling you everything. Remember, we need to reveal those perhaps hidden reservations. Body language is a science that has great depth, and studies and research on the subject are vast. Once you start to delve into body language interpretation, it can become obsessive. You have been warned! We are only going to focus on the areas relevant to our profession—sales!

From my research on Internet sites, one thing astounded me: the human body is capable of producing 700,000 different movements ((*Hartland and Tosh Guide to Body Language*, 2001, Caxton).

Remember, body language is not an exact science, and no single body language sign is a reliable indicator.

Understanding body language involves the interpretation of several consistent signals to support or indicate a particular conclusion.

Let's have a look at some body language movements that I feel are relevant to sales and evaluate their interpretations.

ACTION	INTERPRETATION
eyes looking right	creating, fabricating, guessing, lying, storytelling
eyes looking left	recalling, remembering, retrieving "facts"
eyes looking right and up	visual imagining, fabrication, lying
eyes looking right and down	accessing feelings
eyes looking left and up	recalling images, truthfulness
direct eye contact (when listening)	attentiveness, interest, attraction

eyes widening	interest, appeal
blinking frequently	excitement, pressure
tight-lipped smile	secrecy or withheld feelings
biting lip	nervousness, tension
nail-biting	frustration, suppression
slow head nodding	attentive, listening
fast head nodding	hurry up, impatience
head tilted to one side	nonthreatening, submissive, thoughtfulness
head forward and upright	interest, positive reaction
head tilted down	criticism
head down (in response to a speaker or proposition)	negative, disinterested
crossed arms (folded arms)	defensiveness, reluctance
gripping own upper arms	insecurity
one arm across body clasping other arm by side	nervousness (usually in women)

something held in front of body (handbag, newspaper)	nervousness
quick raising of the head while lowering the eyebrow	what do you mean?
palms up or open	submissive, truthful, honesty, appealing
palm(s) up, fingers pointing up	defensive, instruction to stop
palm up and moving up and down as if weighing	striving for or seeking an answer
fingertips and thumbs touching each other on opposite hands ("steepling")	thoughtfulness, looking for or explaining connections or engagement
interwoven clenched fingers	frustration, negativity, anxiousness
thumb(s) clenched inside fist(s)	self-comforting, frustration, insecurity
rubbing hands together	anticipation, relish
touching nose, while speaking	lying or exaggeration
pinching or rubbing nose, while listening	thoughtfulness, suppressing comment

picking nose	daydreaming, inattentive, socially disconnected, stress
pinching bridge of nose	negative evaluation
ear tugging	indecision, self-comforting
chin resting on thumb, index finger pointing up against face	evaluation
neck scratching	doubt, disbelief
hand clasping wrist	frustration
hands in pockets	disinterest, boredom
crossed legs, sitting—general	caution, disinterest
legs crossed, standing (scissor stance)	insecurity or submission or engagement
ankle lock, sitting	defensiveness

Note: actions and interpretations from www.businessballs.com/body-language.htm

There are many body movements that project the silent language, and we have only covered a very small percentage. It is well worth taking the time to research more interpretations, but be cautious. If you start to delve too much into it, it can become obsessive, and it will quickly take over your presentation. Just because someone has quickly darted his or her eyes away from you might not mean he or she is lying. He or she could have simply seen a distraction behind you, like a quick movement in the background. Don't become so focused on your prospect's body movements that you forget your sales skills. Don't allow yourself to miss key verbal information. Don't stop actively listening. Never allow yourself to become totally confused as to which to believe—the body or the mouth.

This is why I have only listed the key sales interpretations and kept it simple. This is exactly what you need to do, too. The time to check your prospects' body language is when they are answering key questions or closes. If you read confusion, you can reclarify your point. Just be aware of his or her body movements, and check it out occasionally during your presentation to notice any switch of moods. Some interpretations are obvious, like your prospect glancing at his or her watch one too many times.

Use body language at a glance during your presentation to point you in the right direction, if needed. Body language in sales should be used in this way and not to look for some deep dark deception in your prospect with every move he or she makes. Keep it light, and make it work with your presentation. This will allow you to form a good all-around judgment of where he or she is at and focus on any particular areas that may need extra attention or clarifying.

THE OVERVIEW

Before you dive into all the amazing benefits of your product with your prospects, remember, some of them may not have a clue about it, some may know something about it, and others deem to know everything about your product or service. Respect this; people don't like to admit they know nothing about what you're offering (they might feel embarrassed).

It's important to give a general summary of what you're offering before going into the nuts and bolts of how it specifically works. This allows the prospects to form a picture or framework of what your product or service can provide. The overview should be brief, and include any credible notes or awards worth mentioning that the product has proudly achieved along the way.

There is nothing more boring to the prospect than hearing you droning on and on about the history of your product (unless he or she specifically asks.) Sure, give a summary of its history in brief. That's the key here; keep it light, short, and to the point. A great summary can be said inside of two or three minutes. You can refer to this as an "Elevator Pitch," as it should be able to be said during the time it takes to take an elevator ride.

Sales is all about fluidity, transparency, and understanding; the overview should flow in and out of your pitch with these three traits.

Always introduce the overview before going into it.

"Not many people know about us, where we came from, and where we're heading. Have your heard anything about our company?"

Using this style of introduction, you are easing any embarrassment by informing your prospects that don't know, that it's fine not to know. You are also allowing those who know something about what you do to speak up and tell you what they do know. Finally, those who deem to know it all can show off and spurt it all out.

As transparent as that sentence appears, it is *very* powerful. You can gather information about how much your product has been researched by the prospects. Encourage them to elaborate, as you may find some hidden objections or some negative opinions they've encountered upon researching your product. On the lighter side, they may have found some great feedback, too. We need to collate as much information from our prospects as possible.

To divert a little here, if your prospects have found negative opinions about your product or service at this point, don't handle or try to answer it there and then. Never ignore it, but don't react to it. Thank them for it, and advise them that you'll go into that a little later. Here's a good answer to cover it at this stage:

"Thanks for that, John, that's the reason I asked you the question, to find out what you already know or have heard, and I will cover the issue you've mentioned shortly. First, may I ask you, what car do you drive? (replies, rather confused) Do you like it? (Yes, it does the job fine.) Great, tell me, would you ever go on an Internet forum and say how great or fine it is? (No, it does the job, and I can't be bothered.) Like most people, John, OK, now let's say the car you bought broke down the day you bought it, the back up service from the garage was lousy, and no one cared at all; would you then go on to an Internet forum and complain? (Yes). Of course, like most people would. The fact is, there are thousands of people driving the same make of car as you and happy with it, just like you, who don't need to go on a forum and complain. Usually, Internet forums only show the negative side of a product from a disgruntled existing client, not the praises from the thousands of happy clients. I'm not saying our product or service is flawless, what is? However, our aftercare service is outstanding and here to assist in any way we can. We are all human beings, and we will never satisfy 100 percent of the people 100 percent of the time, even though we will always strive to and continue to better ourselves. We always welcome opinions to ensure this happens."

A short statement puts things into perspective and allows you to continue your overview with confidence and a happy prospect, knowing you've acknowledged his or her issue and will address it shortly.

Once the feedback from the prospect has been exhausted, you can then proceed into the body of your overview. I'm going to use a timeshare product for my example, but you can adapt this to any product or service.

"Exectravel has been around for ten years, and we have over 100,000 members. In 2008, 2009, and 2010, we were awarded the prestigious "Best Travel Accommodations" trophy by Globaltime Travel, an independent travel advisory company. The concept is simple, it's like owning your own private luxury holiday villa, but instead of going to the huge expense of owning it fifty-two weeks of the year and the responsibility that goes with it, you only buy the amount of actual time you'd spend in it; perhaps two, three, or four weeks. Also, unlike an outright holiday home purchase, you're not tied to one destination all the time; you can use your purchased weeks in over two thousand fantastic resorts spanning seventy destinations worldwide. All the accommodations are fully furnished and serviced daily, so you can enjoy all the benefits and freedom of self-catering with all the services of a five-star hotel included. When your holiday ends, you don't have the worry or responsibility your outright ownership brings during your absence. To join, there is a simple one-off joining fee and a yearly subscription that covers the maintenance and upkeep of the resort to ensure the quality remains for years to come."

Make sure you write down your company summary and learn it by heart. Get really comfortable and confident, so you never miss a word and can deliver it with ease at will. Reciting it should be as easy as reciting your own name.

Once you deliver an overview like the example, your prospects will have a clear understanding of what you're going to talk about for the remainder of your presentation. They can fit the specific pieces you're going to explain in detail to the big picture.

VALUE, EXCITEMENT, AND URGENCY

VEU are three key ingredients that should be included in every presentation, as they are the three elements that encourage a prospect to buy right away. Far too often, potential buyers walk away to "think about it" because they didn't see the value in what you were offering or they were not excited enough to sign or the urgency didn't create enough fear of losing it if they didn't take it right away. Let's take a look at each component in more detail, and make sure they have maximum affect every time.

VALUE

Some sales professionals insist value is the main reason prospects buy. If I was given a coin for every time I've heard, "If you show the value of your product, the prospect will buy," I'd be a very wealthy man. Although, I agree with the statement to a point; showing value is important, but it is not the only reason prospects purchase.

Take the purchase of a Ferrari or Rolex. The clients who bought one of those products didn't buy based on the value. If value was that important to them, they'd have looked for something a little less expensive that does the same job. They bought it because it makes them feel good. There are exceptions to the rule; however, because to many prospects, value is very important. Each prospect will have a different idea of what good value is or means.

Value does not mean the cheapest. Value is what someone is prepared to pay for a product he or she feels is a fair trade for hard-earned cash. With this in mind, we need to demonstrate that our product or service is made to our prospect's needs. The prospect should feel it makes a positive, beneficial difference in his or her life. The only way to do this with success is to hit and exceed the hot buttons of what the prospect is looking for at a price he or she is prepared to pay or a higher price he or she can afford to pay.

Smart questioning is the solution to discovering your prospect's hot buttons as we looked at in chapter seven. The questions we ask will provide us the information that is important to our prospect's buying decision We must then highlight those points to the prospect during our presentation, demonstrating how what we have to offer matches (and exceeds) his or her demands.

When prospects are answering your questions, you'll begin to get a picture in your mind of what they're looking for. Should key features of your product match what they're telling you, don't interrupt them in your uncontrolled excitement and say something like,

"We can do that!" and blurt out the benefits of what you have to offer. Stay in control, and be professional; never interrupt the prospect, as mentioned previously, because you could cut off a piece of information vital to the purchase decision.

Dig deeper with your questioning and ask why it's important to them. The more information you have, the better you understand your prospect and his or her key needs and why it matters. Once you understand the reasons behind his or her initial answers, you can present a much more personalized presentation that really fits his or her criteria. Once you do this, the value of what you're offering increases.

When you're presenting your product, make sure you get good and positive responses from your prospects and what you are saying makes sense to them. Small closing questions will do this very effectively.

"Does that make sense to you, John and Mary?"

These smaller closes (ABCs) should be increased to a big-value close at the point of reaching one of their hot buttons of importance. Always remind them of what they said previously before presenting your product's specific benefit.

"John and Mary, you told me earlier of the challenges you faced trying to keep your backyard secure so your grandchildren don't run out to the busy main street, yet, you wish to have easy access in and out for yourselves without the need for several locks, right?" (Then go ahead and explain the features/benefits and ease of your product that allows them to have exactly what they need, eliminating the hassle they're currently experiencing.) "Can you both see the value in that?"

You must get your prospects to *buy* the value for themselves; it's not about you telling them. They must feel the value and see themselves enjoying the benefits. The words you use, and the way you explain the usage, will create this.

Never use yourself as an example when demonstrating value.

"The reason I bought it myself..."
"I see the value because..."

Always use past clients (third-party stories) who have had similar situations or circumstances to the prospects, as they will relate better.

"Peter and Jane, my last clients had exactly the same situation as yourselves. They purchased, as they saw the value in having this one lock because it not only replaced the..."

Ask your prospects what value they see in what you're offering.

"Based on what I've shared with you so far, John and Mary, what value can you see in this for you?"

These sorts of questions will allow your prospects to talk freely about how they perceive the value of what you're offering. It is their explanation, using their own words. This will also give you a guideline to the scale of where they're at in relation to the value you're trying to project.

On a final note about value, you should also get a feel as to the monetary value your prospects are putting on what you are offering before you show the price. This will demonstrate how well you've done in showing value.

"OK, John and Mary, time for a little game; based on everything we've spoken about and the benefits this will bring, would you like to take a guess on the price?"

(This will either come as sweet music to your ears or a complete shock!)

EXCITEMENT

Excitement is something that drives many prospects into purchasers. It's the thrill of owning it. Some people who buy in excitement do so regardless of value. Prospects can get caught up in the magic of it all through an excitement purchase, even though they have no need for it and had no intention of buying it. How many times have you heard friends say, "I have no idea why I bought it!" It's usually excitement that's to blame.

Some save money for years to buy something that excites them; a fast car, unique vacation, expensive watch, and so on. These are calculated consumers, and they know most of the time it will devalue or probably end up with no value at all. Yet, they buy because they simply want it, regardless. They can be a sales professional's dream prospect.

Unfortunately, we hardly see any of those types, so it's up to us to get them excited about what we have to offer. Used correctly, excitement will close the sale there and then. It is a powerful human emotion that can trash any form of logical thinking.

Take bungee jumping, base jumping, and all those other extreme dangerous sport activities. Why do people do it? The thrill, the excitement, and the adrenaline it creates, certainly not the logic!

Excitement needs to be in sales, but selling on excitement alone is not good for you or the prospect. Excitement soon fades. Your prospects will soon be looking at the receipt for the return policy. Then will come the call to your office: "We've been thinking about our purchase, and unfortunately..." This then causes you disappointment.

You must always back up excitement with logic and substance.

Imagine a beautiful dress being displayed in the shop window. The shape of the mannequin keeping it in place brings out the best features of the dress. If you remove the mannequin, it falls to the floor and looks like a mess.

Always make sure there is a mannequin underneath your sale to give it substance after the excitement of the initial purchase has faded. That way, the purchaser can always see the real reason he or she bought it in the first place and buyer's remorse is kept at bay. In sales, our mannequin is value and logic.

Pride of owning is a good place to start when creating excitement. Prospects need to feel good about what you're offering.

Creative and descriptive words contribute to excitement. Think about the excitement that a child feels when he or she is told he or she is going to the most popular theme park in the world. Think of the anticipation, as his or her parents tell him or her of all the great things he or she is going to experience and the characters he or she is going to meet. In most cases, the build up to the vacation is more exciting than being there. The magical descriptive words create the greatest image in the child's mind, and this makes the excitement.

It's the same in sales. Using creative, descriptive words will form a clear, perfect image in your prospect's mind, and it will be unique to only them, as mentioned earlier. Once again, the correct questioning will provide the information you need to create excitement with your prospects.

Choose your words carefully, avoiding boring, mundane words like "nice" or "lovely." Be creative, and bring the scene or situation alive with the words you use. A picture should be easily formed in your prospect's mind.

Use the human senses as a guide to your descriptions: smell, touch, sound, and vision, like the aroma of fresh-roasting coffee, the sound of the tide lapping against the shore, feeling the tropical, balmy, warm breeze against your skin, etc.

You can use creative, descriptive words to energize any product or service. They create an anticipation and desire in the prospect that leads to excitement. Refer again to what he or she told you previously when you asked those relevant questions. Descriptive words and imagery create incredible excitement when conversing with prospects about their hot buttons.

URGENCY

Urgency is used to either create a fear of loss emotion in your prospects or an incentive to purchase. Done correctly, it is simply too good to wait or reject. Used correctly, it can make the sale immediately, instead of them walking away to think it over.

Industry uses urgency all the time; marketers thrive on it. How many times have you seen some of the following slogans in department stores or on TV?

"Last few available."

"Sale ends tomorrow."

"There's a 60 percent discount on everything today only."

"Call right now, and receive a second item absolutely free."

Perhaps some of the best examples of creating urgency are demonstrated on live TV shopping channels. The image of the presenter is usually accompanied by a digital banner surrounding him or her, showing the number of units left available and the airtime left for that product. It continually counts down as people phone-in to buy. This very visual banner is pointed at several times by the presenter, along with his or her persuasive, descriptive, and urgency-filled pitch that goes something like:

"If you take a look at the top left side of your TV screen (presenter points), this is how many Egyptian Cotton Towel Packs we have left. To the top right of your screen is the amount of time we have left on this fantastic offer. Whichever gets to zero first, ends this one-time offer. Get dialing, we only have thirty-seven left, and thanks, Mary from London, for your order." (Purchasers' first names and city they called from are scrolled along the bottom of the screen.)

"Look at the quality (touches the towel close up), pure, 100-percent Egyptian cotton. Soft, rich, luxurious. How good will they feel to you? Get dialing, only twenty-three left..."(Buzzer sounds, and lights flash in the studio. The presenter looks surprised.) "Oh, you know what that means. The next eight people to call will get a second pack absolutely free; what an amazing offer. Quick, dial right now. There's only thirty seconds to go!"

I think you get the picture.

Urgency only works if your prospects like what you are offering. It's no good trying to create a fear of loss or an incentive to purchase now if there's no real interest. You never know the interest level of a prospect when you first meet them. It takes smart questioning and deep digging to get a real understanding of them. Our objective is to get them to see themselves using what we're offering and seeing the benefits and value of the purchase. Once we feel our prospects are at the point where we can ask for the business, it is no good bringing in urgency at that point.

Creating urgency is not something that should be left to the very end of your presentation; it sounds desperate and salesy. It could really affect your credibility from the prospect's point of view. Urgency should be dripped throughout your presentation from the start. It should be transparent and very clear to your prospects. Don't overdo it, as you'll scare them off, and they won't believe you.

Here's some good examples of introducing urgency at the front end of your pitch.

"The model you have picked out is a very popular, Mary, great choice. Let me tell you a little about it. I'm not too sure if we have that color left, but I'll check later if you're interested; however..."

"That's a very demanding time of year, and I'd certainly need to check the availability. You might need to consider alternative dates. How many people would be traveling?"

"Just to let you know, we have a fantastic promotional offer just for today, and it really is amazing; you'll love it. Four people already purchased today because of it. We'll go into what it is at the end, but first, let's see if you like and can use what we're offering."

Reference to your first urgency statement should be made a couple of times in the midpoint of your presentation, when you know the prospects are really becoming open to the idea of the great value and benefits your product has for them.

"As you've just told me, you can see the benefit of its portability, Mary. I must say again, I do need to check the availability on this, as it is a very popular choice."

Urgency shouldn't be the reason for buying; it should be used to assist your prospects in the decision process of buying today instead of tomorrow. Just like excitement, if someone buys on urgency alone, it is without substance and likely to cause remorse from the purchaser the following day.

The urgency close is also a great way to ask for the business and make the sale at the same time. For this to work, your prospects must like what you're offering, see the value in it, and have the excitement of potentially owning it. They must be aware of the costs involved and show it's comfortably affordable.

"That's great, John and Mary. As mentioned, I need to make a quick call to check the availability. To qualify for the 20 percent discount and free fitting, I will need to confirm the order on the same call. So, if they have that model in red and can fit it next week, I'll go ahead and place the order?"

Remember, urgency is maximized when there's excitement, and excitement is created by prospects seeing great value. You need all three ingredients for it to work effectively.

ASKING FOR THE BUSINESS

M any prospects don't buy because they simply are not asked to. This may seem absurd and baffling to many sales professionals, but it is a fact. We can practice and perfect all the sales skills in the world and spend hours working on our attitude, but that will all come to nothing if we don't ask the prospects to buy.

After an entire presentation, closing every door and demonstrating all the benefits as to why the prospects should buy (and getting them to agree with your points), you get to the "point of sale." The point of sale is where all your hard work comes down to the yes or no; it's that crucial point.

However, to many, it should be renamed as the "point of crumble." Some professionals can flow fluidly through a presentation and form great relationships with prospects until the very end. All the hard work has been done, yet to so many, asking for the business is the hardest part of the presentation.

It is sometimes painful to watch that stand-off moment when the sales professional ends his or her final word of the pitch and stares at the prospects in silence with a smile of expectation. The prospects then look at each other in silence, then back at the sales professional with a look of confusion. The sales professional, still silent, raises his or her eyebrows, leans forward a little, waiting for a response from the prospects. Finally, the confused and now embarrassed prospects break the silence and tell the sales professional they need to go away and think about it.

The sales professional assumed the prospects knew he or she was at the end of his or her pitch, and the silence and smile that followed was asking them for a buying decision. They didn't; why should they? They were never verbally asked.

We need to understand why this happens so many times in all fields of sales. There are two main reasons. First, some professionals don't know what to say. And second, there is a fear of rejection. Knowing what to say is probably the easiest to overcome, having the courage to do it and overcome the fear of rejection is another.

Let's look at the sensitive area of fearing rejection. This is very common, from those new in sales right through to the more seasoned professionals.

We need to understand why there is a fear of rejection. It could be you don't want to accept failure, or that your job is target related and your numbers aren't the best. Perhaps, and probably the most popular, you fear confrontation with your prospects, risking your relationship with them. Whatever the reason, you should know yourself what it is. There is one common factor they all have; the fear will affect your sales efficiency, and it must be dealt with for you to succeed.

Let's take this into perspective; if you don't ask, you don't get! The majority of prospects you meet don't really know what is expected of them. They are usually with you to get information and maybe a comparison of what you're offering to that of your competitors. It is fair to say most of them have no intentions of buying from you on that occasion. With the professionalism, advice and relationship you share with your prospects, you have earned the right to ask them for a buying decision; there is nothing wrong with that.

It is unfair of prospects not to expect you to ask them to buy, after all, you are there to promote your product or service; you are a professional *sales consultant.* Is it so shocking for a doctor to recommend a treatment following a consultation? Or a dentist to shy away from telling you that treatment is required following a checkup? Of course not.

You are a professional, you earn your money through selling your service or product; be proud of that, and don't be afraid of rejection. Not everyone will say no when you ask for the business. One thing is for certain: everyone will say no if they are not asked directly.

With this in mind, what do you really have to lose? You never know how prospects will respond when you ask them to buy. They might just surprise you. Over the years, so many sales professionals are amazed and stunned when certain clients they never expected to purchase do so when asked to buy. It just takes a little courage. The first few times you ask for the business are the hardest. After a few times, you'll ask for the business without even thinking, and it will become very easy and feel unnatural not to do so.

Let's take a look at the knowing what to say. We need to make this process as transparent and natural as possible. Like closing, it needs practice, so you become confident and comfortable in your delivery.

The last thing you need at this delicate and crucial part of your pitch is your personality to change, projecting a nervous, anxious, and desperate sales executive. Also, don't change to become a stern, serious, and intimidating monster. This will definitely influence the prospects in their judgment of you and your offer.

Instead, continue in exactly the same way you've been presenting, but get to the point, and make yourself perfectly understood.

Here are some great ways to ask for the business:

"So, John and Mary, you like it?" (Yes). "And is that down payment comfortably affordable to you?" (Yes). "Great, welcome as my newest owners!"(Stretch your hand out to shake theirs.)

As an assumptive close:

"It's great you can use it and see the benefits. I'll need to take a down payment; how much would be comfortable affordable to you?" (They answer.) "Fantastic, congratulations on your purchase." (Shake hands.) "Let's get the paperwork done."

You could even do a conditional close:

"So, what you're telling me, John and Mary, is if we could do it for that price and install it for free, you'd go ahead and sign right now?" (Yes). "We have a deal. You'll be delighted with your new purchase." (Shake hands.)

Or, simply:

"Would you like to buy it?"

Ask for the business in your own way, using your own personality, but make sure you ask for it.

There was a great story I heard about a certain fast-food chain that had problems selling their hot apple pies. Top people were assigned to come up with a strategy to find a new way to increase pie sales. The solution was simple and multiplied tenfold the number they sold.

"Thank you for your order, would you like a hot apple pie with that?"

Success, simply by asking for the business!

THE FOUR PILLARS OF SELLING

Each and every one of us is distinctive, and we have individual personalities with strengths and weaknesses in different areas. This makes us unique; it configures who we are and gives us character.

Our born traits definitely influence our personality when it comes to selling. Some approach prospects with logic and hard closing, while others are more empathic and sell with emotion.

Some sales professionals try to master every sales skill in the book and have all the closing techniques down to a fine art but still have difficulty getting the business and fail to understand why. Being a professional consultant will bring you success in sales; however, this alone will never make you great in sales; it takes more. Your sales approach to the prospects makes the difference. I'm not talking about attitude and other personal attributes (although vitally important!), I'm talking about creating a sales balance.

The sales process must have a good balance. If we looked at a group of sales professionals, each would have his or her own style of selling. Some may prefer the hard approach, based on strong closing techniques and pure logic. Others may be empathic, preferring the softer "I'm your best friend" technique. Some rely on generating excitement and urgency to make the sale.

There's merit in all of these techniques and all highly effective, that is, if they are used proportionally throughout the presentation. The challenge comes when only one is used.

Your personality will naturally lean you toward one of the selling traits (emotion or logical) as it will be more in your comfort zone. You'll either feel more comfortable selling emotionally or with logic.

Sales styles can be broken down into four types: emotion, logic, urgency, and product. Each should be used throughout your presentation proportionally to create a balance and not be one-sided. As professionals, it's up to us to identify which side of the scale we prefer to sell from and add balance to it.

If you have too much emotion in your presentation, then there's usually not enough logic and reason to do it today. If you have too much logic and urgency, then there's not enough emotion in your pitch, and it appears too pushy and hard selling, as your relationship building is somewhat lacking.

Below is a diagram that I refer to as the "Four Pillars of Selling," along with an explanation of what each pillar represents.

PRODUCT KNOWLEDGE (Why Choose My Product)	SALES SKILLS (Buy Today)
RELATIONSHIP (Buy Me)	LOGIC (It Makes Sense)

EMOTION   LOGIC

PILLAR ONE: RELATIONSHIP (EMOTION)

This represents the emotional side of your presentation. It is all about forming a relationship/friendship with your prospects. This gains their trust and confidence in you as a person. It has nothing to do with business. There is no logic needed, no sales skills, and requires no product knowledge. It is the art of conversation and well-implemented body language. Relationships require the ability to form rapport quickly and listen actively. It requires empathy and contribution wherever and whenever needed. Timing is crucial, and it's not what you say, it's how you say it that matters. Relationship building and strengthening continues throughout your presentation, not just at the beginning.

PILLAR TWO: PRODUCT KNOWLEDGE (EMOTION)

This represents why your prospects should choose your product over a competitor's. You must know everything about your product or service. You should know where and when your company started, by whom, and how it has developed. Your research should also include where it's heading. Know the positives and the negatives; check out Internet search engines for forums to read what customers are saying. Know the inner mechanics, so you are ready for any question. Don't wait for others to train you on product knowledge, take personal responsibility, and check it out for yourself. As professional consultants, we must know our trade and our tools inside and out. Keep an eye on developments in your company and product updates; don't get left behind. Your prospect views you as the CEO, so make sure you live up to that reputation.

PILLAR THREE: SALES SKILLS (LOGIC)

This represents your ability to allow your prospects to buy today rather than tomorrow. They guide the prospects through your sales strategy, gaining commitment and clarification along the way. Sales skills allow you to handle objections and reveal any hidden concerns your prospects may have. Used correctly, sales skills are transparent and simply a natural series of questions to assist the prospects to reach a purchase decision. Sales skills are also a tremendous benefit to you. They allow you to see where your prospects are "at" throughout your presentation. This gives you notice of whether you need to change direction or make additions to the rest of your presentation.

PILLAR FOUR: LOGIC (LOGIC)

This pillar is the ability to show your prospects that to purchase makes sense. It is pointing out your product's features and benefits through a series of facts. These facts should be presented in solution form, based on the challenges your prospects have already told you. If done correctly, your prospects should feel that to purchase your product is the logical solution; you are, after all, using their own words. Logic is the extreme opposite of emotion; it is calculated and definitive. Logic is done periodically throughout your presentation to back up your answers factually and give solid reassurances to objections.

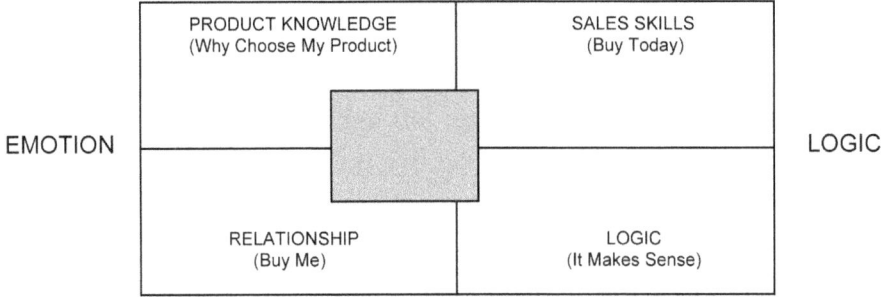

NOT ENOUGH REASON
(ABOVE DIAGRAM)

People who sell with this type of emotional ratio will find it difficult to get the "sale on the day." They focus way too much on their relationship and empathy with their prospects. They restrict or fear using sales skills and logic. This makes creating urgency and asking for the sale today difficult. It can also make the transition from friendly chat to talking business challenging.

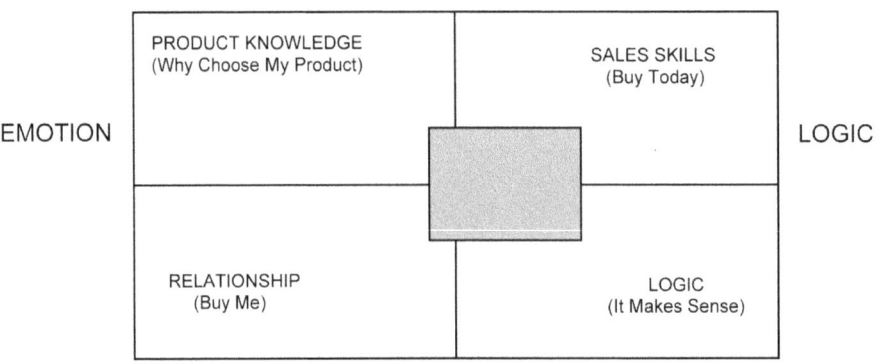

TOO HARD SELL
(ABOVE DIAGRAM)

People who sell with this type of logical ratio will most likely scare prospects off or suffer from far too many cancelled orders. It is "too hard sell," as very little bonding with the prospects has been made, and there is not enough confidence and trust from the prospects. They will feel they've been forced into the sale instead of being allowed to buy.

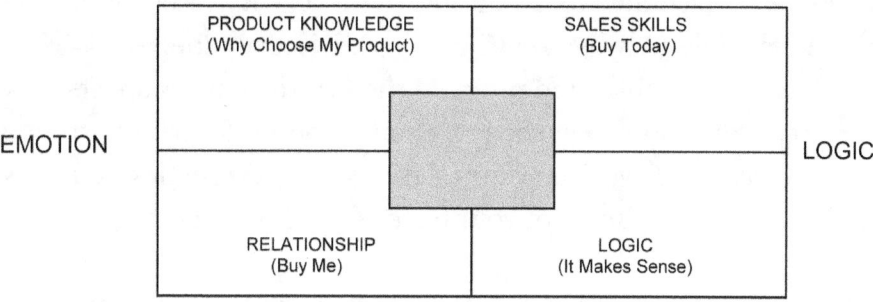

IDEAL
(ABOVE DIAGRAM)

Perfect! The right balance has been demonstrated by making a friend of the prospects and gaining their trust. The product knowledge has earned confidence, and it makes logical sense that it's the right product for them. Finally, there's just the right amount of sales skills to allow the prospects to buy it now.

Once you have identified your preferred style of selling, whether that be more toward the relationship side or the logical side, you need to make the balance. Successful selling as a professional consultant requires you to make great relationships with your prospects but also demands you must have the confidence to use sales skills and logic to make the sale happen.

Never change your personality, and use the side you lean toward to your advantage, as this is where your natural strength sits.

However, learn to develop and incorporate the side that you don't feel comfortable with—the balance. Get out of your comfort zone, and try new things.

If you're an empathic seller, practice sales skills, and use them. If need be, replace the word "closing" with "clarify." Remember the same principle (Always Be Clarifying). Discover the reason your product makes sense, and promote the fact to your prospects. Ask for the sale, you have earned it. Should you prefer selling from a more logical side, work on your relationships. It is costing you sales and the reason for some of your buyer's remorse clients.

There are not many who can achieve absolute perfection with an equal balance in the four pillars of selling, and that is not what is expected. Just make sure you move further over to the side that you're lacking in your presentations. If you do this and practice until you are comfortable and confident, you will generate more solid sales.

PUTTING IT ALL
TOGETHER

O ur primary goal as a professional consultant is clear: make the sale.

There may well be secondary goals, too, such as the collection of referrals or future repeat business strategies, but foremost, get the sale. The secondary goals are usually there to set up future clients to achieve the primary goal again. To attain any goal, there needs to be a plan of action. This plan must include a strategy on how to get the primary goal accomplished.

Take a look at any environment that is goal oriented, not just sales. In soccer, they pay coaches huge sums of money to create winning strategies to attain the primary goal: win the championship. Every week, they carefully analyze the team they are going to face next.

They look at how they play, who their key players are, where their weaknesses lie, and many other factors that could influence the outcome. They look at their own team's strengths and how they can maximize them against the opposition. Out of this research, they create a game plan, the steps the players need to follow to win the next game. These week-by-week game plans are designed as the necessary steps needed to be followed to attain the primary goal.

If things are going wrong on game day, at half time, the coach usually insists the players stick with the game plan or only slightly modify. They are that certain, they know it'll come good in the second half, and for the team that created the best game plan, it usually does.

Coaches do not look ahead to the championship, only to the next game. They know the only way to the championship is through winning every next game. Keep winning the next game, and the championship comes to you. It's as simple as that.

It's important to have goals, but without a strategy, they are difficult to achieve. This just leads to frustration and disappointment. In sales, to achieve our primary goal, we need to have a strategy. A game plan that we stick to, one that we can rely on, believe in, and that works. This gives us confidence even before we meet the prospects, as we know exactly what we need to do.

As every prospect is different, we need to have a strategy that has a solid foundation with some flexibility. A path that can be followed every time with every prospect. This path should be a template, a sort of one-size-fits-all mold we can wrap around every prospect we meet that allows us to then tailor-make it to fit them personally.

For this to happen, we need to create a structure or process. A series of steps for us to follow as a guide for what comes next before reaching our primary goal of getting the sale. Like the soccer coaches I mentioned, each step of our structure is like next week's game to them; it needs winning before going on to the next step.

Many sales companies have their own structure or sales process. The following I'm using is an example of one (mixed with mine), with similar steps I've used at one time or another at different companies I have worked with, but all of these are extremely effective. Some of the steps you may be familiar with but by different names. The point is, you need a structure to be successful in sales, and the one below is the most effective example I know and use.

Some of the following steps may not be relevant to your area of sales (telesales, for example), so take what you need, and leave what you don't. Think about your product or service, and apply your own structure. It should have a front-end strategy (relationship building), a mid-strategy (your pitch), and an end strategy (asking for the business). *Make sure you have one; you need a game plan to win in sales.*

These are areas we have already covered, so I'm not going into great detail, simply demonstrating the structure in which they are applied.

1. MIND-SET AND ATTITUDE

It all begins with you. Get your mind-set and attitude right. Ditch any negative thoughts before you meet or talk with your prospects. Focus on the positive, and get the winning mentality. Believe in yourself and the work you've done to get you to this point. You know the product, you've got the sales skills, you're looking sharp, and ready to go.

Believe prospects are going to buy, and this is your next sale. Belief is stronger than doubt.

Get in the zone, and remember that you choose your attitude, not the other way around.

Take a look at Internet search engines for "Motivational Quotes" just before meeting prospects. Having a positive hit is fantastic as the last emotion you absorb before meeting them, and it's energizing.

Your mind-set and attitude need to be 100 percent before you move on to the next step.

2. FIRST CONTACT

You never get a second chance to make a first impression.

Prospects will form a picture within seconds of meeting you, and even before that. They'll have already started the moment they saw you walking toward them.

Make sure you get this right. Be professional in your appearance; it's the first thing they'll notice. Get your clothing right and be smart. Check your shoes, are they clean? Dirty shoes can reflect in your attention to detail. Your clothing may be professional but will be quickly undermined if your shoes don't shine.

What about your personal grooming, are you tidy? How's your hair, a crow's nest or neat? If you look as though your were out until four in the morning, they'll notice that instead of your professional wardrobe.

Dirty hands and fingernails? This is tremendously important, as you'll be presenting your hand to them in a few seconds. How would you feel if someone reached out with stained, flakey, blackened, chewed, fingernails to shake hands?

Clean teeth or stained from coffee and tobacco? Your smile is the first thing the prospects see in your attempt to form a relationship with them. Nothing is more off putting than a smile that makes them think your teeth are made from wood.

Good eye contact or distracted? When you are approaching your prospects, make good eye contact with them, and don't make them wonder if it's you who's going to see them or not.

Smile while you approach, and reach your hand out to shake his or hers. Make it a firm handshake, not soft and weak. Don't break from his or her hand, and show your sincerity from the start. Weak handshakes are often perceived as insincere.

Just before you shake hands, make sure you have met the right people. As you approach, their body language should tell you if they're your prospects or not. To be safe and polite, say their names with a questioning intonation:

"Mr. and Mrs. Smith?"

Always use their last names, if this is the first time you've spoken with them; it's a great sign of respect. Say their names with a smile. When they acknowledge you, they might say it's OK to use their first names.

"John and Mary, please..."

That gives you permission from then on to use their first names. If they don't say it, stick with the Mr. and Mrs. for the initial stages.

Introduce yourself and what you're there to do.

"I'm pleased to meet you. My name is John Smith, and I represent ABC. I'm going to be looking after you today and assist in any way I can."

Best only to use your first name if you wear a name tag.

Engage in some light, transparent chit chat, nothing to do with business (how they got here, weather, etc.). After about a minute or two, excuse yourself for a moment, and leave them alone briefly. When you return, you are no longer perceived a stranger. In your absence, your prospects can comment between themselves about their first impressions of you. If you've got it right, they may say something like, "He/she is not what I expected. He/she is really nice." This is the first big step in the prospects accepting you.

These types of comments are exactly what you need for the first impression. They give you the foundation needed to build a solid relationship. As the first sale that is made is you, congratulations, with those comments, they're on the way to buying *you*.

It is human nature to form opinions of people in an instant, and this will never change. As professional consultants, we need to accept this and adapt. Never give prospects a reason to have a less than perfect first impression of you.

3. MAKE A FRIEND, LEARN THE LINGO

Steps one and two are really about digging the trench for the foundation of our structure, and step three is about filling it with concrete to make a solid foundation to build on. People won't care about you until they know how much you care about them. Get in their "group;" it's that straight forward. Use the techniques I described in chapter five.

Relationships make sales, so make a friend. Too many sales executives skip this critical stage, either because they are too impatient to get to the sale, or they simply can't be bothered.

Encourage prospects to talk, and make sure you're using open questions and managed silences. Remember, they are probably nervous, and it is our job to make sure those nerves disappear. This is done by allowing them to see our genuine sincerity. Your empathy, active listening and interaction will either strengthen or weaken your relationship, as it is constantly being perceived by your prospects. It's amazing how many times you'll hear prospects say, "I can't remember the name of the last guy we spoke to."

That is the impact the person before you had—zero. The prospect couldn't even remember the person's name, and in most cases, if you asked the prospect to describe what he or she looked like, the prospect probably couldn't even do that.

How in the world could the person before you stand a chance of getting those prospects to buy? It would never have happened, as the sales executive couldn't be bothered to build a relationship with them, and the prospects couldn't be bothered with the sales executive or what he or she had to offer.

The art is knowing when to get on with it, and make sure you don't cut corners and bore them. Keep an eye on responses and body language. If they become fidgety and start to give shorter responses, move on. Invest your time in being interested in your prospects, and it will pay off.

The relationship development continues from here until the very end, and it does not stop.

4. THE INVESTIGATION

It's time to be the consultant here. From now on, you need to find out what's important to your prospects, and discover where their hot buttons lie.

Use the great questioning techniques we mentioned in chapter seven. Make sure you make your questions relevant, and don't forget to dig deeper where needed. The use of open questions during this part of the process is crucial. If you have a prospect who is particularly quiet, make sure you manage your silence. Actively listen while he or she is talking, and as previously described, never interrupt or try to finish his or her sentences. Allow the prospect to elaborate, or if need be, make him or her elaborate by using the word "why" in your responses. Make sure you listen to everything he or she says; the prospect may just mention or hint at something worth perusing and important to the buying decision, so don't miss it.

Remember to be sincere with the prospect when he or she responds. Be empathic when needed, and if he or she is describing a challenge, imagine how you would have felt if it would have been you. Doing this effectively will improve and strengthen your relationship.

Stay focused, and think about every question you ask. Have a goal in mind. Where do I want to go next? *Think*! Has the prospect answered my question enough, or do I need to dig a little deeper? Can I now show him or her what the product will do for him or her personally. Do I have enough information to demonstrate the *value* personally? Do I have enough information to get the prospect *excited* using the hot buttons just told to me? Am I able to create *urgency* with the information I've gathered so far?

When you are happy that you gathered enough information, give your prospects a brief (thirty seconds) recap of what they've told you. This demonstrates you've listened and totally understand their needs. Finish with:

"Have I just summed up everything that's important to you? Is there anything else I may have missed that you wish to tell me?"

Without a thorough investigation, there is no way you can do a personalized presentation. The more corners you cut here, the more you cut your chances of making the sale, as you will simply be telling and not actively catering to their needs that allows them to buy.

5. THE OVERVIEW
Time to put the product summary into play as discussed in chapter thirteen.

This really is the transition from getting to know your prospects and finding out what they consider important to actually showing them what your product will do for them.

You must practice the overview until you can recite it from memory with the same words every time. Make sure you write it first, and read it over until you are happy it is clear, concise, and to the point. Learn it, and get confident and comfortable with it.

The overview should last no longer than two or three minutes, especially if your investigation stage went on a little too long. Your prospects will probably want you to get on with it by now. Be to the point when you present the overview, maintain good eye contact, and check your body language; don't fidget or rub your hands together. Stay relaxed and composed, and maintain open body language.

Always start your overview with an introduction to it, something along the lines of, "Before we discuss the actual ins and outs or the workings of (your product), let me just give you a very brief general overview; it will help to give a better and bigger picture…"

When you've finished your overview, always end with:

"Does that make sense, John and Mary?"

Never use phrases like:

"Do you get it?" or "Do you understand?"

These sorts of phrases are very condescending and can insult prospects.

6. WHAT'S EXPECTED OF YOUR PROSPECTS

You need to let your prospects know exactly what's expected of them. They also have a part in this process and should be informed now.

Depending on your field of work, you should know the time frame you're expected to work within to have made the sale. Some industries expect the deal the same day, while others allow you to work prospects over time. If you are self-employed, maybe working from home, then set deadlines and targets for yourself. This helps with goal setting and time management.

This stage should be like the overview, a brief explanation of what's going to happen, so there are no surprises at the end of your presentation.

Perhaps you have an incentive for them to join today, or maybe you need to reappoint them at the end of your meeting for a follow up. Whatever limits you have, you need to let your prospects know what they are.

If you have a purchase incentive for them to buy right after your presentation, tell them you have one, but don't tell them what it is. This could lead to questions that curb the flow but something that you will deal with toward the end of your presentation.

They know what is expected of them. Sure, you may get an objection if you want the business right after your presentation, but don't react and get into an arm wrestling match.

"I respect your views on not making a decision today; however, on occasion, there is a good and intelligent reason to do so. Remember, it's also fine to say no. It may not be for you, and you might not like it. The only thing I ask, John, is you keep an open mind and first see if it makes sense and you can use it. Is that OK with you?"

It is imperative you *use your own words* that are *relevant to your company/business.*

You must get out of your comfort zone and be confident and comfortable with it by practice. Once the prospect knows what's expected of him or her, he or she will feel better, and so will you.

7. THE PRESENTATION—HOW YOUR PRODUCT WORKS

This should be totally personalized using information from the investigation stage. Mold your product or service around what the prospect told you. Don't make the mistake of doing all the talking; you must use open and closed questions throughout this step.

Get *regular* feedback from your prospects.

"Does that make sense?"
"Is this something that you feel you can use?"
"Based on the information I've just shared, how would this benefit you?"
"Can you see yourselves using this?"
"Can you see the value of it? How?"
"Would this make your life easier?"

Once again, never use phrases like:

"Do you get it?" or "Do you understand?"

Even though you are in an explanation stage of the process, you are still consulting and still strengthening your relationship. These sorts of open questions allow the prospect to buy and not make him or her feel like he or she is being sold to. The prospect must tell you the personal benefits to them, not you simply pointing them out.

The questions you ask are more important than the answers you give. Make sure they are goal-oriented ones, and know why you are asking them. Think of the answer you would like to hear from your prospects, then form a question to attain that response. You need to create value, excitement, and urgency, and this comes from the questions you ask and the attitude on how you respond. Your attitude needs to be fueled with enthusiasm, and the words you use need to paint amazing pictures. Get with them. Put a spring of excitement in your voice. Drizzle your sales skills all the way through your explanation.

Once you've finished this stage, make sure it really makes sense to them. Remember, don't be caught by "nodding dogs" who are just agreeing with you for the sake of it, as mentioned in a previous chapter.

Finally, ask at the end (modify these questions to make it relevant to you field of sales.):

"Does it make sense to you?" and "Can you see yourself using it?"

These both need closing fully before you go to the final step.

8. ASK FOR THE BUSINESS
Refer to chapter fifteen for specifics on how to ask for the business.

FINALLY
Putting it all together takes practice, and you need to treat sales as your profession. The more you put in, the more you get out. Sales is about continual performance improvement and trying to better yourself every time. There is no graduation in sales. If you're going to mess up, mess up, and learn from it. A mistake is never serious unless it is repeated.

Don't fear rejection. Learn something from every prospect you meet.

One last thing to try if all else fails:

"Well, it's been great meeting you, and I enjoyed our time together. One last thing, what would it have took for you to buy today?"

or

"What would you need from me to make you say yes today?"

You never know, the prospect may just say something you can agree to do!

JUSTGOSELL.COM

A FEW FINAL THOUGHTS

B elow are two topics I have encountered during my time in sales and would like to share my thoughts with you; they are subjects I have included at www.justgosell.com.

IS SALES A NUMBERS GAME?

Sales closing technique—do they work? Or is sales success simply a numbers game?

Sure, if you had a line of a million people, and you asked each one, "Would you like to buy this?" then you'd probably expect a percentage to agree. However, if sales is indeed a numbers game, then why do top performers exist?

Anybody who considers sales to be a numbers game is, on one hand, correct, as what we know for sure that in sales, we do need to see the numbers for us to sell anything. On the other hand, relying on the numbers to create the sale will result in missing out hugely, as what we don't know is which of the numbers buy.

Treating sales as a numbers game is an insult to those top performers who strive to reach higher levels. They understand there is no graduation in sales and continually push themselves to improve their sales performance.

They do this by staying one step ahead, and they dedicate time to research their product/service thoroughly. They keep themselves up to date with what's happening within their industry, both good and bad. Top performers strive to better themselves by perfecting their sales skills and professionalism.

They treat their prospects with respect and understand the importance of giving 100 percent focus and effort to their current number and not to save it for the next number. Sales success doesn't come from your next prospect, it comes with the one you're currently with.

The reason they are top performers is that they understand the need to perfect their sales craft to identify the numbers who buy. By doing so, they also turn non-buying numbers to buying ones as their commitment to sales excellence pays off.

THE RECESSION

Since 2009, twenty-four-hour news channels, newspapers, radio, and the rest of the world's media have forced us daily, hourly, and even to the minute to listen or read about the "financial crisis," "markets in despair," and "recession to get worse!" Their words were being backed up and echoed by huge financial investment corporations being interviewed "live" on primetime slots.

Let's look at this a little closer. Media corporations are a business, right? They did not set up as a registered charity. They went into business to make profit, just like every other profit-driven organization. The big twenty-four-hour news channels are broadcasting every day and night to make their shareholders happy.

Keeping the shareholders happy requires a cycle. The way media channels make money is mainly through sponsor advertising. The sponsors invest based on numbers tuned in to the media channel. The way the media channels maintain and increase their numbers is to *sell* their product effectively. *Reporting the news* is one thing, *selling the story* is another.

Remember the live coverage of the Iraq conflict? Or the Afghanistan conflict? Media reporters yards away from the frontline, with explosions, fire, chaos, and gunshot sounds beamed directly into our homes, as it happened.

The reports from the studio of how it could lead to the next world war or "If this happens or that happens, it could lead to disaster on a global basis." These sorts of slogans and statements terrified many people watching, as they feared the "What if..." comments might come true. The media did its job; they sold their story as millions tuned in to see the latest developments.

It is the same with the financial crisis. They are selling a story: the reason they went into business. As for the financial investment corporations going on the TV to report doom and gloom; isn't that great free advertising for them? "Come and see us, we'll help during this time."

I'm not saying there's no economic downturn at the moment. There have been losses of jobs and hard times. However, didn't this happen twenty-five years ago? And before that? and before that?

Question; from 2009 until today, have people completely stopped spending? Are shopping malls completely empty? Has not one person or company prospered during this time? Has no one taken a vacation since 2009? Has not one house been sold or purchased since then? Has no one been promoted or a company expansion been reported since 2009? Have the stock market values not had an increase since then?

The fact is, even through the toughest of times, people spend. Value becomes important to more people, and they may tighten their belts somewhat, but they still buy. Vacations are taken, presents are bought, cars are upgraded, and restaurants used.

Let me ask a question, what would happen if the media stopped reporting the recession completely? What would happen if the "What if..." speculation from the media stopped tomorrow? Take nothing away from the media, they take a piece of news and sell it extremely effectively.

The challenge is, even some sales professionals buy into the media pitch. They can lose focus on the sales process, give up easier on prospect objections, and lose their positivity—easier to blame the "recession" than their lack of effort and determination.

Prospects today have a great non-buying pact excuse. "Oh, the recession..." Some sales professionals buy it or react to it (just as bad). Think about this the next time you're with a prospect. Does he or she still have a house and job? Did he or she come to see you?

Probably. The recession is being used as an excuse by many as a smokescreen not to purchase.

Successful sales professionals remain successful because they treat this objection just like the daily objections they hear (selling the house, kids in college, etc.). They remain totally focused on the sales process.

They show the value of the product by showing the cost of not buying. They ask smart questions to open up their clients. They find the thread they require to create a need from the prospect. They make a friend with the prospect to gain trust.

The reason top performers continue to achieve today is they are simply better than the media at selling.

Top performers don't ignore reality, they simply adapt.

(This blog was written in 2012 and was referring to the global recession in 2008/2009.)

FINALLY

Thank you for taking the time to read this compact book, and I hope you took something from the topics I've shared.

Log on to my website www.justgosell.com, and keep up to date on sales training, and share some of your ideas, too.

Happy selling, and never give up!

—Colin

ABOUT THE AUTHOR

Colin Knowles has worked in sales for more than twenty years and has exceeded required targets in multiple industries, including timeshare, financial sector, outside cold marketing, and electric sales. An expert in face-to-face selling, podium selling, and telesales, he was recognized as the top sales closer worldwide by one of the leading brands in the global timeshare industry and has shared his know-how to help other sellers achieve similar success.

While still active in direct sales, Colin has also held multiple management positions and has been responsible for training, mentoring, and coaching sales people. As a professional sales coach he has conducted independent sales seminars for both general admission and individual organization audiences with various coaching needs as well as personalized one-to-one coaching.

Colin and his wife Jennifer currently reside in Spain, where they own a sales and business consulting company. He also owns JustGoSell. com, an online community for sales professionals to share their best practices and develop their sales skills. *Just Go Sell!* is his first book.

www.ingramcontent.com/pod-product-compliance
Lightning Source LLC
Chambersburg PA
CBHW051512170526

45166CB00001B/491